Oracle SQL
Developer Handbook

About the Author

Dan Hotka is a Training Specialist who has over 28 years' experience in the computer industry and over 23 years' experience with Oracle products. He is an internationally recognized Oracle expert with experience dating back to the Oracle V4.0 days. Dan has co-authored seven popular books including the *Database Oracle10g Linux Administration* by Oracle Press. He also authored *Oracle9i Development by Example* and *Oracle8i from Scratch* by Que. He is frequently published in trade journals, and regularly speaks at Oracle conferences and user groups around the world. Visit his website at www.DanHotka.com. Dan can be reached at dhotka@earthlink.net.

Oracle Press™

Oracle SQL
Developer Handbook

Dan Hotka

New York   Chicago   San Francisco
Lisbon   London   Madrid   Mexico City   Milan
New Delhi   San Juan   Seoul   Singapore   Sydney   Toronto

Oracle SQL Developer Handbook

1234567890 CUS CUS 019876

ISBN-13:   978-0-07-148474-9
ISBN-10:   0-07-148474-4

Sponsoring Editor	**Proofreader**	**Illustration**
Lisa McClain	Carolyn Welch	International Typesetting and Composition
Editorial Supervisor	**Indexer**	
Jody McKenzie	Valerie Robbins	**Art Director, Cover**
Project Editor	**Production Supervisor**	Jeff Weeks
Carolyn Welch	Jean Bodeaux	**Cover Designer**
Technical Editor	**Composition**	Jeff Weeks
Sue Harper	International Typesetting and Composition	
Copy Editor		
Bob Campbell		

Contents at a Glance

Contents

PART I
Getting Started

PART II
Using SQL Developer

PART III
SQL Developer Reports

PART IV
Appendixes

Foreword

Back in the late 1980s when I started with Oracle, I remember typing commands into SQL*Plus and having to be so careful about not making a mistake. I soon learned how to use the SQL*Plus command editor and could make powerful corrections in the editor. At some point I learned about the edit command and was very excited when I learned how to set my own editor (like notepad, ed, or vi). This was back in the days of the vt220 terminals and emulators. One of my first "large scale" projects involved 50 concurrent client/server users, all running on a 286 processor that ran Xenix. SQL*Plus certainly became our friend on that project. All of our reporting used RPT. If you think you have it rough developing with the tools that are available today, go back and try to read (let alone write) an RPT report.

At some point in the world of development, along came a free tool that closed a much-needed gap. The tool had a name that made you laugh and a sound byte to go with it. The tool was none other than TOAD. TOAD was an open source (or freeware) tool before we knew what open source was and how it would change the software world. For years TOAD dominated the market because of its ease of use and people's love of (and need for) freeware.

Oracle once again is changing the software world with their open source entries and support. People can't figure out Oracle's strategy in this world. To me it's quite clear. Oracle's new competitor? None other than SQL Developer. Once known as project Raptor, this new tool is both free and rich in functionality for both developers and DBAs in today's complex Oracle environment.

I highly recommend this book by Dan Hotka. He has authored numerous books, and in this case has written a book that will help you really understand SQL Developer. In addition, he provides excellent user group presentations and in general is a wonderful person. Best of luck with SQL Developer and keep on making a difference every day!

—*Bradley D. Brown*
Chairman and Chief Architect, TUSC

Preface

Oracle SQL Developer (referred to as SQL Developer throughout this book) is an Oracle RDBMS SQL and PL/SQL development environment. This tool is developed and supported by Oracle Corporation as a useful tool in the development and maintenance of Oracle-based applications and database objects.

SQL Developer allows the user to create and maintain database objects (such as tables, indexes, and relationships); view and maintain data; and create, maintain, and debug PL/SQL code. With its intuitive and uncluttered GUI, this tool greatly simplifies development tasks.

Installing SQL Developer

SQL Developer runs on Window, Linux, and Mac OS platforms. Installation is as simple as downloading and uncompressing (unzipping the download file) into a folder. Database connections can use the JDBC thin drivers or SQL Net (names server or TNS Names). These connections are stored with or without passwords in the navigator tree for easy access to the users' common database connections. Using multiple connections, SQL Developer makes it easy to access code and data on various Oracle instances.

Using SQL Developer

SQL Developer is a GUI tool designed with the developer in mind. The interface is intuitive, and there are useful options in any context within the tool. The navigator tree structure of the tool makes database objects easy to find, as shown on the following page:

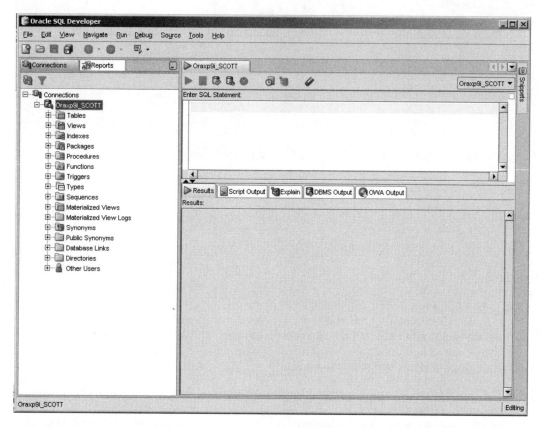

The SQL worksheet supports SQL, PL/SQL, and a selection of SQL*Plus commands. The SQL window has a history to save the user's work, code snippets that allow the easy drag-and-drop of available SQL code, PL/SQL code, and optimizer hints to quickly aid in productivity.

Simply navigate the tree to find the object you desire to work with. The SQL window allows the user to create and maintain SQL; query results and explain plans are displayed in the lower pane. Many function keys, right-mouse clicks, and drag-and-drop operations enhance the user's productivity.

SQL Developer allows for easy data display, export (even creating Excel spreadsheets), and manipulation by simply clicking a table name.

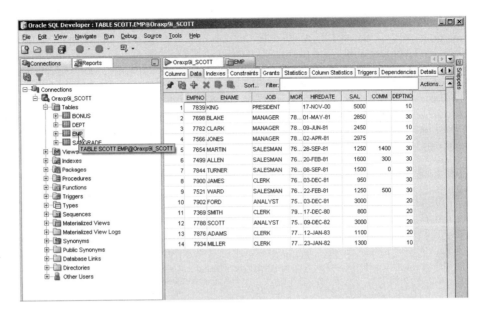

SQL Developer makes it easy to create DDL scripts of just selected objects or for an entire schema. SQL Developer also makes it easy to create test data that is associated with these objects in the DDL script.

SQL Developer is a full-featured PL/SQL editing, debugging, and run-time environment. SQL Developer allows the user to use a PL/SQL editor to create PL/SQL procedures, functions, triggers, and packages with ease. Right-click any of the objects shown here to access the New <object type> Wizard. The New Procedure Wizard sets up the basic code syntax for the user according to the parameters filled in from the wizard.

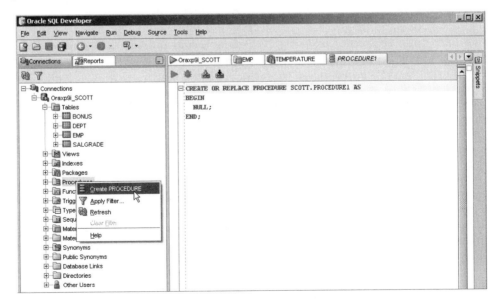

The PL/SQL editor has the same code templates and code assistants as the SQL window environment.

SQL Developer allows the user to execute any PL/SQL procedure, package, or function, allowing for the input of any run-time parameters and input variables. Output is easily displayed and saved.

This same PL/SQL editor is also a full-featured PL/SQL debugging environment, which allows the user to step through individual lines of code, step over subroutines the user is not interested in debugging, run the code until the cursor is reached, set break points, set conditional break points, watch variables, watch the contents of cursors, and change the contents of variables on the fly!

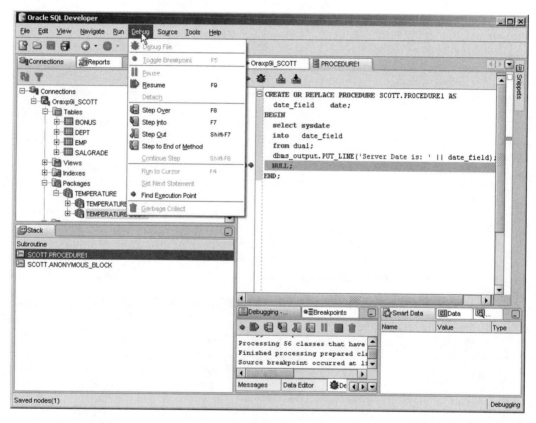

SQL Developer contains a rich set of reports that allows the user to easily see useful information about the database environment that they are connected to. SQL Developer will show detailed information on just about every aspect of an Oracle database instance: from the database parameters, to detailed session information, including SQL cursor contents, to tablespace utilization, and more. The following illustration shows the major categories of reporting available in this version of SQL Developer. SQL Developer even allows the user to add reports (his or her own SQL scripts) to this reporting environment.

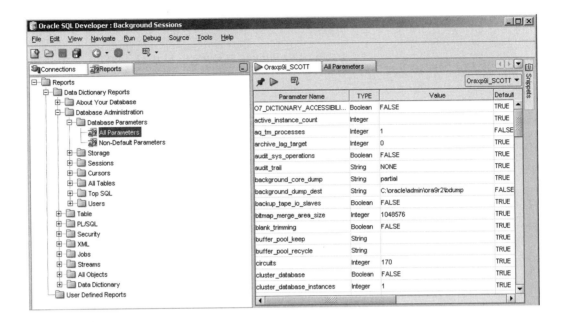

Third-party tools are available to embed into SQL Developer. These tools include database monitoring, spell checking, and more.

This book covers every aspect of this new and powerful development tool from Oracle Corporation. I hope you find this book useful in discovering all the features available that are designed to enhance your Oracle development productivity.

Acknowledgments

I recently crossed 28 years in the computer industry. My career has been a fun ride with few regrets. I have friends at most of my stops along the way. I have witnessed first hand the considerable change in speed, capacity, and size of both computers in general and the computing environment as a whole. I have witnessed similar changes on the software side of things as well (from punched cards, to character-mode green-screen terminals, to the advent of windows and multitasking workstations, and to today's interactive web-based multiple-host applications). SQL Developer is a perfect example of how Oracle Corporation has adapted to the needs of their user community—in this case, the needs of the developers who work closely with the Oracle RDBMS.

A special thanks goes to Gail, my wife of 28 years. Her patience, love, and understanding have allowed me to take on opportunities such as writing and the travel that comes with my line of work. She has been the perfect partner for this ride we call life. My family (Elizabeth "Libby", Emily, and Thomas) continue to give me the strength to fuel my continued success in life.

I am truly blessed with the many friends and business associates who have helped mold me both as a person and in my professional career. You are too numerous to list here and I would fear leaving someone out.

I would like to take this opportunity to thank a few people who I believe have helped to mold my professional career that I still enjoy today.

I have asked Bradley Brown to do the foreword for this book. I met Brad years ago on the trade-show circuit where we both continue to frequently speak. Brad has been my business mentor on my latest self-employment training/consulting adventure. He has kept me focused, especially through the trying times of a start-up business. He continues to be a valuable resource to me for business direction and training ideas.

I continue to utilize the talents of many individuals. These folks have gone out of their way to answer my technical questions, provide me with industry insights, and assist me in about any way they can. I first wish to thank Kevin McGinnis. If it were not for his PC and networking skills (and volumes of patience!), I would not be able to provide the quality on-site training that I am able to do. Other technical advice has been gleaned from (in alphabetical order): Steve Adams, Steve Blair, Bradley Brown, Rodney Dauphin, Daniel Fink, Tim Gorman, Jonathan Lewis, Russ Lowenthal, Rich Niemiec, Robert Nightengale, and Bert Scalzo. Thank you for your technical assistance through the years.

I want to thank those managers who have helped mold my career into the success that I continue to enjoy today: Karl Lenk (Sperry-Rand, Inc.), Gary Dodge (Oracle Corporation), and Deb Jenson (Platinum Technology, Inc.).

I want to thank Lisa McClain for working with me on this book and on other Oracle Press writing opportunities. I want to thank Sue Harper of Oracle Corporation for her time and involvement with this book to make sure that I accurately covered all of the features of SQL Developer.

And finally, I wanted to be sure to thank my extended family for their years of support. I extend a special thanks to my parents Philip and Dorothy; my in-laws Dean and Marian; my siblings Mike and Janice; my sister-in-law Sarah; and my grandmothers Mamie and Gladys, who will always have a special place in my heart.

Introduction

Oracle SQL Developer is a feature-rich development tool for the Oracle RDBMS environment. Feature-rich generally means "difficult to learn," but this is not in the case with Oracle SQL Developer and its intuitive navigator-style interface.

SQL Developer was developed to enhance the productivity of the developer or power user, displaying useful information with the click of a mouse, easing the pain of typing long column names, or the drudgery of researching where a column is used throughout an application. SQL Developer takes the pain out of syntax lookup with an available wizard right off the navigator interface that easily allows for any database object to be created. SQL Developer also contains code examples and subroutines that allow for easy code development. Sometimes functionality is not obvious and all of the features of SQL Developer are not fully utilized because the user is unaware that these features are even available.

The *Oracle SQL Developer Handbook* is intended for any user, and at any level of experience, to get started quickly and gain insightful knowledge of this new and exciting tool from Oracle Corporation. There are many features that are not obvious or would not be utilized without the comfort-factor gained from working through an example from a practical illustration.

Part I of this book contains the Product installation (Chapter 1), Getting Connected (Chapter 2), and Quick Start (Chapter 3). These chapters are designed to help the reader get SQL Developer installed correctly and quickly, illustrate the various ways of establishing connections to the Oracle database environment, and provide enough detail so that the novice user can be productive with SQL Developer in a short time span.

Part II of this book focuses on SQL Developer's main interfaces. Chapter 4 shows you how to use the SQL Developer interface and how to customize the various displays to maximize productivity. Chapter 5 focuses on working with the Database objects—each of the objects supported by SQL Developer is introduced, their Create Object wizards are reviewed, and the various informational displays associated with each object are illustrated. Chapter 6 covers the SQL Worksheet interface and all the features associated with it. Chapter 7 provides in-depth information on the PL/SQL Code Editor, primarily the PL/SQL coding and debugging environment. There are features such as snippets and code insights that are not obvious by just clicking around SQL Developer. Chapter 8 then ties up various loose ends associated with database objects and code that are not covered in previous chapters.

Part III covers the extensive number reports, reports that cover literally every aspect of the Oracle application database environment, that are available in SQL Developer. This section wraps up with just how easy it is to add your own reports to the SQL Developer interface.

The appendixes include keystroke/function cross-references and additional SQL Developer code extensions or plug-ins to enhance SQL Developer productivity.

I hope you find this book useful in your day-to-day work with the Oracle Relational Database Management System. Thank you Oracle Corporation for providing your user community with such a functionally rich tool for their Oracle productivity needs.

—Dan Hotka
Author/Instructor/Oracle Expert

PART
I

Getting Started

CHAPTER
1

Product Installation, Upgrades, and System Requirements

QL Developer is supported on many popular workstation platforms. This chapter
will illustrate the installation process, describe how to install future versions and
upgrades, and list the minimum system requirements for SQL Developer.

System Requirements to Include Supported Databases

SQL Developer is developed using JDeveloper IDE. Your workstation platform will need to
support this level of Java. SQL Developer for Windows does have two download options: one
with the JDK 1.5 Java environment already installed and one without. The one without makes for
a much faster download, which is useful for product updates. The Linux and Mac OS versions
require a working Java JDK 1.5 environment.

SQL Developer supports and is certified for Oracle Databases versions 9.2.0.1, 10g, and later.
SQL Developer also supports Oracle 10g Express. Certification means that all the SQL Developer
features will work with these releases of the database.

NOTE
*SQL Developer is not certified for databases earlier than 9.2.01;
however, many users still working with Oracle 8.1.7 do use SQL
Developer. Certain features do not work on 8.1.7.*

SQL Developer requires a working Java JDK 1.5 environment. The Windows version of SQL
Developer can be downloaded with an installed JDK 1.5 environment if your system does not
already have one installed. The Linux and Mac OS platforms need to have the Java 1.5 environment
installed and working prior to product installation, as shown in Table 1-1. Table 1-2 shows the
hardware requirements for SQL Developer.

NOTE
*Table 1-2 contains the documented system requirements. My
experience is that SQL Developer works fine on my classroom PCs
that are Pentium II machines running at 300 MHz with 196MB of
RAM.*

Operating System	Required Java Environment
Windows	JDK 1.5: download the version with JDK 1.5 already installed from www.Oracle.com.
Linux	JDK 5.0 Update 6: download from: http://java.sun.com/j2se/1.5.0/download.jsp.
Mac OS X	J2SE 5.0 Release 3: download from: http://developer.apple.com/java/download/.

TABLE 1-1. *SQL Developer Java Environment Requirements*

Operating System	Processor	Memory	Disk Space
NT, SP 6a Windows 2000, SP 4 XP, SP 1	Pentium III 866 MHz	256MB	42MB with JDK 1.5 110MB without JDK 1.5 (installed with download)
Red Hat Linux v2.1, 3.0, or 9.0 SUSE SLES8	Pentium III 866 MHz	256MB	110MB
Apple Mac OS X v10.3	1 GHz G4	256MB	110MB

TABLE 1-2. *SQL Developer System Requirements*

Installation Process

SQL Developer can be downloaded from www.Oracle.com. Click Downloads and then SQL Developer. The direct link to the SQL Developer home page is http://www.oracle.com/technology/software/products/sql/index.html. Figure 1-1 shows the various SQL Developer options available on the SQL Developer home page. Notice all the information that is available.

NOTE
This web site has frequent changes; Figure 1-1 is merely an example of the type of information that is regularly available.

The SQL Developer files are in a compressed format. Use WinZip on Windows, Folder extract on Windows XP and Mac OS X systems, and Uncompress on Linux/Unix. WinZip is available from www.winzip.com (see Figure 1-2).

NOTE
There was not room in the screen shot for the Mac OS options. These options are: 28.9MB disk required; double-click the SQL Developer icon.

Installing and Running SQL Discoverer on Windows

Create a folder and unzip or extract (Windows XP) the contents of the download file into this folder. Double-click the SQLDeveloper.exe program in this folder.

TIP
I put a shortcut on my desktop that points to this program.

Installing and Running SQL Developer on Linux

Create a directory and uncompress the SQLDeveloper.zip download file into this directory. Run SQL Developer with this command: sh sqldeveloper.

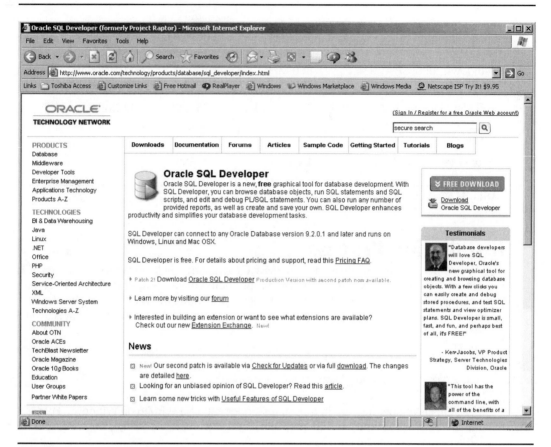

FIGURE 1-1.   *SQL Developer home page*

Installing and Running SQL Developer on Mac OS

Create a folder and unzip the contents of the download file into this folder. To start SQL Developer, double-click the SQL Developer icon.

NOTE
Check the SQL Developer home page for the installation guide that will have more tips and techniques if you have a unique computing environment.

Installing Newer Releases

You have two ways to update SQL Developer. SQL Developer is designed to download and update only modules that have changed. This process is started from the Help | Check For

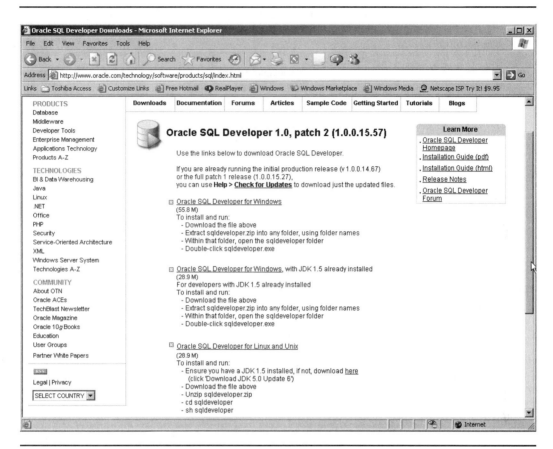

FIGURE 1-2.   *SQL Developer download site*

Updates menu item. Making this selection will start a wizard that will allow you to select the type of update you want to do and from which Oracle download site to retrieve the updates.

The other way is to simply download the entire new download file. Before extracting or installing the new download file, be sure to export your connections! Once installation of the newer version is complete, import these connections to preserve your existing database connections. This is easily accomplished by right-clicking Connections in the navigator tree and selecting Export Connections. Be sure to save this export file to a location other than the SQL Developer folder.

It is recommended that you remove the contents of this folder (simply delete the contents) and unzip/extract the entire downloaded file. After starting the updated SQL Developer, simply right-click the Connections navigator item and select Import Connections to restore your various connect strings.

NOTE
SQL Developer does not have an Oracle home, nor does it use the Oracle Installer process for installation or deinstallation. When upgrading or removing SQL Developer from a system, simply delete the contents from the folder that it was originally installed into.

Product Versions

SQL Developer's version and build information can be displayed from the menu item Help | About. The Extensions tab will show any updates that have been applied. Oracle Corporation has been regularly releasing newer versions of SQL Developer. The release notes available on the SQL Developer home page will always contain useful information about new features and updates covered by the release.

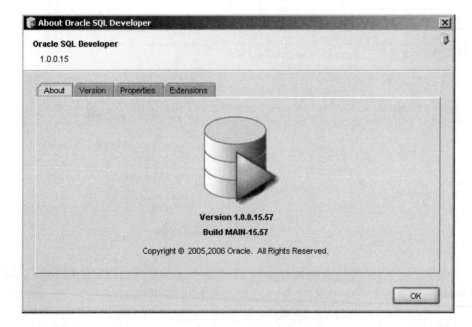

Getting Help

SQL Developer has a robust help system that contains a table of contents, full text search, and an index. There is a lot of useful information on the SQL Developer home page such as release notes, tips and techniques, and installation guides; you can even join and ask questions on the SQL Developer Forum (see the next section).

Join the List Group

SQL Developer has a forum that you can join. This forum will allow you to review the questions and answers posed by other SQL Developer users. Frequently, the SQL Developer development staff will post answers to the questions.

Simply click SQL Developer Forum on the SQL Developer home page to access the forum. Figure 1-3 shows a sample of the SQL Developer Forum activity.

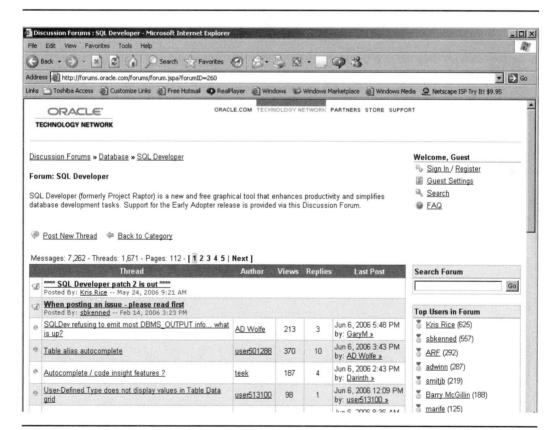

FIGURE 1-3. *SQL Developer Discussion Forum*

Summary

This chapter illustrated the hardware and software requirements needed to run SQL Developer. This chapter documented how to download both SQL Developer and the required Java environments required to run it. This chapter reviewed how to access the download files, how to retrieve updates to the tool, and where to find additional help and support.

CHAPTER
2

Getting Connected

QL Developer is a robust development and query tool that connects to and works with the Oracle database. The Oracle RDBMS maintains user identifications and passwords, and allows access to data and privileges to various database resources (such as the ability to create or change objects or to change data). SQL Developer will perform only actions that its user ID has permissions to do. SQL Developer stores this user ID and connection information—necessary to find the host computer, Oracle listener process, and ultimately the Oracle database—in database connection descriptions, which may be called simply connections.

This chapter will show you how to create and maintain database connections in SQL Developer. SQL Developer uses these connections to simplify connecting to various databases with the click of a mouse. SQL Developer can export these connections and import them, which is useful when upgrading SQL Developer or when sharing common connections with other SQL Developer users.

Working with Connections

SQL Developer uses connections to remember the information required to locate the Oracle database of interest and to provide the login credentials necessary to establish a connection to the database. SQL developer saves all this information and easily displays it in the navigator window, as shown in Figure 2-1. Passwords are optionally stored. If they are not stored, then every time you open a new connection, SQL Developer will prompt you for the required password to complete the Oracle login credentials.

NOTE
These passwords are stored encrypted, but if you are working in a sensitive environment, it might be a good idea not to allow SQL Developer to store passwords at all. Consult your DBA or check with your supervisor for your company's policies on password security.

There are two buttons on the Connections tab in the upper-left corner of Figure 2-1 (shown at the next page). The refresh button reestablishes any open database connections, and the funnel button allows you to filter or display only specified objects within the connection.

Clicking the + sign next to the Connections keyword will display all the connections available. Clicking the database connection name will establish a connection, open a SQL window on the right side (notice the tab with the database connection name in it), and set up the results area for this SQL window (the lower-right part of screen). Connections can also be established by right-clicking the connection name and selecting Connect from the pop-up menu shown here.

If you need to make any changes to the connection information, simply right-click on the screen and select Properties. From here, you can also choose to disconnect from

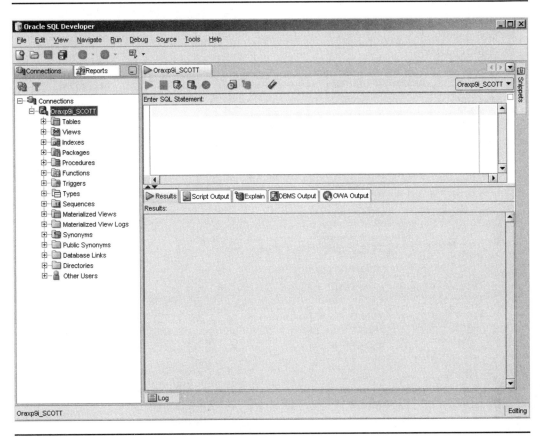

FIGURE 2-1. *Using SQL Developer connections*

the database (i.e., close your connection), delete the connection, or even rename the connection. The other options in this box are discussed later.

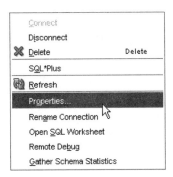

The next image shows the connection information in an interface similar to when the connection was originally created. You can choose whether or not to save the password for the connection, and if the path to the database changes, the new connection information can be easily changed.

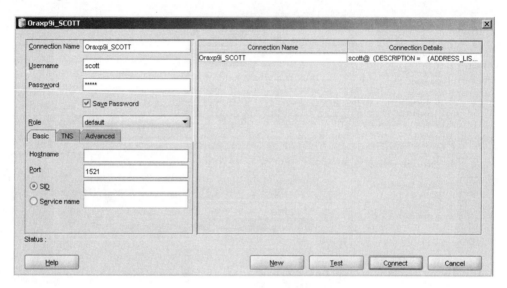

TIP
This feature is useful to add new user IDs and passwords to an existing connection to a database instance. Open the properties of an existing connection to a particular database and change the Connection Name and the user ID (and optionally, the password) to quickly add a new connection to a particular database.

Establishing New Connections

New database connections are easily created. Simply right-click the connections item and select New Database Connection from the pop-up menu.

This will open the New/Select Database Connection dialog box.

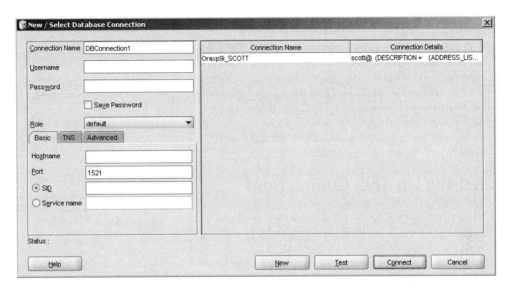

Enter a unique name in the Connection Name box. View the other available connections if there is any question if a connection already exists.

TIP
For the connection name, I like to use the Oracle instance name followed by the user ID. This gives me useful information without having to open the connection to see if that is the database I want to work with. Using the instance name first will also group all of your connections per Oracle instance.

Enter a valid user ID and password. Decide if you want to save the password. The password will not be displayed. After filling in the connection information, you can click the Test button to try the connection information. If you entered the password incorrectly, SQL Developer will let you know. The Connect button creates the connection and connects the user to the database. The New button clears the connection dialog. The Cancel button closes the connection dialog without doing any work, and the Help button opens the useful help text about this dialog box.

There are two roles to select from: default is for normal users, and SYSDBA is for system-type accounts that will have privileges to start or stop the database, etc.

Database location information is defined in one of the three available tabs under the password. You only need to fill in connection information in one of the three tabs.

NOTE
If there is any question as to the connection information that you need, please consult with the Oracle DBA staff. They will have the correct information required to connect to the desired Oracle instance at your site.

Setting Up Basic Connections

The Basic tab allows you to define the host name for the computer that has your Oracle database. You can also put that computer's IP address in this field. The Port number is for the IP port that the Oracle listener is set to listen on. You will then need either the Oracle SID (system identifier) or the Service name.

Click Test to test the connection; the status will appear just above the help button.

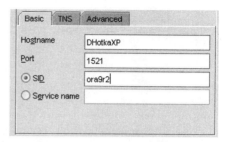

Setting Up TNS Connections

The TNS tab is useful if your company is using TNSNames or Oracle Net to manage Oracle connections. Enter the Oracle Net identifier in the field if you are using Oracle Net. If you are using TNSNames, simply click the arrow in the Network Alias box to display the available TNSNames entries.

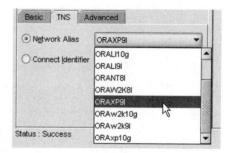

Setting Up Custom JDBC Connections

The Advanced tab allows you to enter your custom Java URL.

Connecting to Oracle10*g* Express

SQL Developer can easily connect to an Oracle 10*g* Express Instance running on the same computer as SQL Developer. The example shown next will use the connection name of Oracle10gXE, along with a sample user name and password. Notice that the host name is 127.0.0.1, the port is 1521, and the SID is XE. The host name "Local Host" can be used in place of the IP address, and the Oracle10gXE connection might be configured to use a different port than 1521.

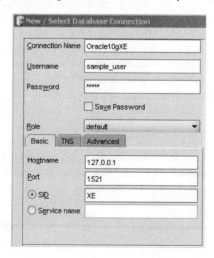

NOTE
*If you are connecting to Oracle 10g Express on a different computer,
substitute the host name of the computer that has the Oracle10g
Express instance or that same computer's IP address.*

Exporting/Importing Your Connections

SQL Developer allows database connections to be saved externally to SQL Developer. This is
useful when upgrading to newer versions of SQL Developer or when sharing specific connection
information with other SQL Developer users.

To export, simply right-click the Connections item to view
the Export Connection Descriptors dialog box, which allows you
to name the export file, select a location (via the Browse button),
and even select the connections to be exported.

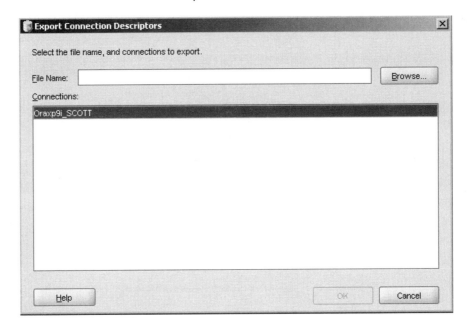

To import connections, select Import Connections from the same pop-up menu used to do the
export. SQL Developer will add any new connections in the file and will replace any connections
that already exist. A similar dialog will be displayed that will allow all or just specifically selected
connections to be imported.

Summary

This chapter illustrates how to create and save database connections. Some knowledge of your
computing environment is required to accurately fill in the required information. Once these
connections are made, simply click the connection name in the navigator window to connect to
the database desired.

CHAPTER
3

Quick Start

QL Developer is an intuitive tool with mouse-clicks, keystrokes, menu items, and function keys to access interfaces, templates, wizards, and code assistants. There is usually more than one way to do the same function. Oracle developers have different skill sets and different coding habits, and SQL Developer can easily adapt to the styles of these various types of developers. This chapter is intended to get the new SQL Developer user quickly acquainted with the tool's main features.

Introduction to SQL Developer

SQL Developer allows you to easily work with SQL statements; scripts that contain SQL statements; and PL/SQL blocks, procedures, functions, and packages. SQL Developer also allows you to create and view the status, data, or associated code with just about any object associated with the Oracle RDBMS that you have privileges to access.

SQL Developer has four major interfaces, depending on what you want to work with. The SQL Worksheet interface is illustrated next. Connecting to the database gives you the main Connections Navigator tree on the left side of the screen. Notice the Connections and Reports tabs at the top of this section. Also notice that you can minimize this navigator window to maximize the SQL Worksheet on the right. The SQL Worksheet allows you to work with SQL statements, scripts that contain SQL, and/or PL/SQL blocks. This area also has a history of SQL statements entered (discussed later in this chapter). Notice the output tabs that contain the SQL statements result set, script output, an explain plan for the SQL just executed, DBMS output, and OWA output.

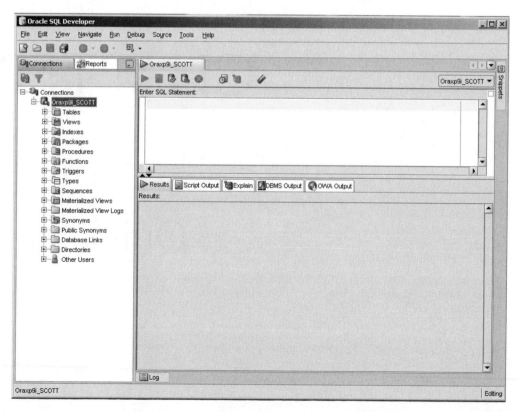

Once a connection is first established, a SQL worksheet is opened with the connection name on the tab. You can open as many connections and tabs (interfaces) as your workstation has memory.

SQL Developer can display a variety of information, including data, for any table object. Simply open the Tables in the navigator window and click a table name. Notice the new tab with the table name and the table information, and the tabs across the top of this Table Display tab, as shown next. You can quickly see the table columns; see and maintain, save, and export the data in the table; view the available indexes, constraints, grants, statistics, column statistics, triggers, dependencies, and details (more statistics and storage details); and even view and save the DDL in SQL format for this table object.

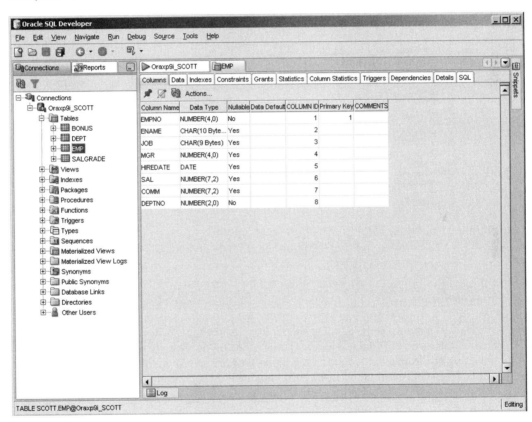

The third main interface is the PL/SQL Code Editor, shown next with boilerplate code. You can create, edit, compile, and debug your PL/SQL packages, procedures, functions, and triggers using this interface.

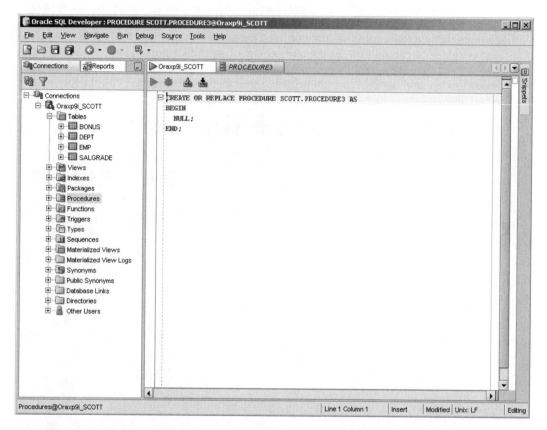

The last interface is the SQL Developer Reports interface, accessed from the Reports tab on the navigator side of SQL Developer. These reports place a variety of useful information at your fingertips. For example, the next image shows Free Space report: the tablespaces and their available space. Part III of this book goes into detail on each available report as well as how to add your own SQL scripts to this report interface.

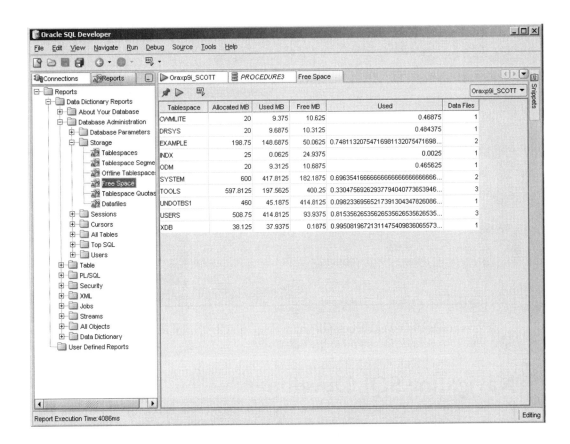

Establishing a Connection to the Database

SQL Developer maintains database connections. SQL Developer does not require a connection to the database until there is a required task or request of the database (such as executing a SQL statement or viewing data). For example, the report selections can be viewed without being connected to Oracle, but once a selection is made, if there is no connection established for this report, then SQL Developer will prompt for a connection to use.

NOTE
The example in this section will use SQL*Net with the TNSNames configuration. See Chapter 2 for a complete discussion on getting connected to the database.

To create a connection to the database, simply right-click the Connections item in the navigator window and select New Connection from the pop-up menu. The next image shows a connection to the database for the user SCOTT using a TNSNames entry of ORAXP9i.

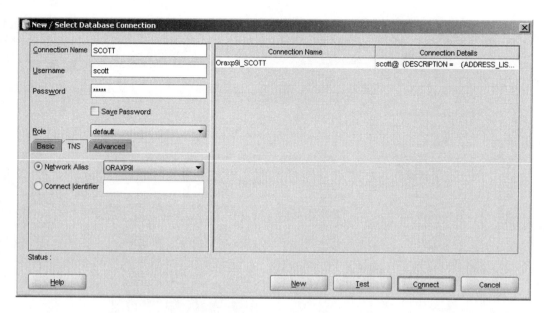

If your connection was successful, you will see a SQL Worksheet interface and tab on the right with your connection name in the tab.

Navigating SQL Developer

SQL Developer is a functionally rich tool. Most features are requested from the navigator window. The menu bar across the top has functions useful across the tool or that will be available for only certain window interfaces. For example, the debug menu items are context-specific to the PL/SQL Code Editor (i.e., are only available when using the PL/SQL Code Editor interface).

The Connections, Reports, Help, and Snippet windows are all undockable. Right-click any of these tabs and select Float to undock these windows from the SQL Developer interface. (Chapter 4 will illustrate all of these features.) You can click and hold on a window tab and move it around the SQL Developer interface. This will give you the ability to split the windows and see information for more than one table or see information about a table while working in a SQL worksheet. You can also right-click the tab and select New Tab Group to view the tabs at the same time. Right-click the tab and select Collapse Tab Groups to put the display back to single-tab display mode.

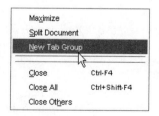

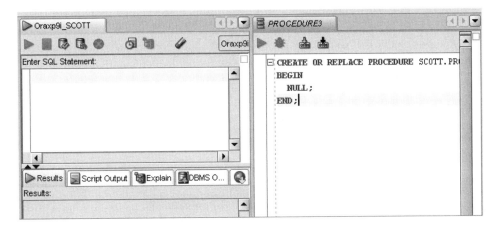

Right-click and select Maximize to undock the window and make it large. This makes coding using SQL Navigator a snap! Right-click the tab and select Restore to return it to its prior size. Double-clicking the tab will maximize it or return it to its prior state as well.

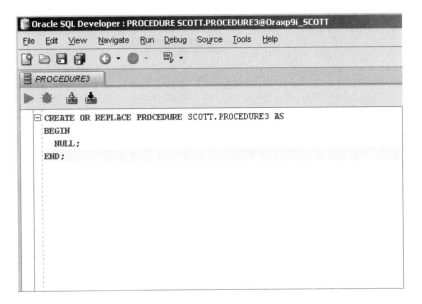

SQL Developer allows you to hide windows and to make windows (like the help system and the snippets) autohide and become available when you move the mouse over their bar on the right side. With the window open, click on the '-' in the upper-right corner to hide the window. You will see an icon along the right side for the window. Hovering the mouse over the icon pops open the window, and clicking the X in the upper-right corner will close the window. If you inadvertently close a window you meant to minimize, simply click the View menu and select the object type you wish to see.

You can right-click most anything in the Connections Navigator window. When you right-click a connection name, a menu allows you to rename the connection, start and connect to SQL*Plus using this connection's connect information, disconnect (close the connection), or open another SQL window.

Right-clicking the Tables node in the Connections Navigator brings up the pop-up menu seen next. Most of the items on the Connections Navigator have the ability to start a wizard that will walk you through building a new object of that type (a new table in this case).

Notice the Apply Filter option here. This appears in many places too, including the Connections Navigator (useful if you have a lot of connections). This filter allows you to display just the object type that meets the filter criteria. For example, the next image is filtering the display on the SCOTT tables. This filtering has the same functionality as the LIKE function of the SQL language. The '%' is the global character, and the '_' skips a position. This feature is very handy when working with applications that have more than 50 objects that would appear in the window. This helps you to find just the objects, by pattern, that you want to work with. To undo this feature, either access the Filter dialog again and simply put in a '%' or select the Clear Filter menu item. If there are quite a number of objects, a Show More item will appear that will display the next set of objects for that particular type.

Viewing, Changing, and Saving Data

SQL Developer allows you to see a variety of information about any of the objects. Simply navigate to the item of interest and click it. For example, the next image shows all the available information, coordinated across the tabs, including the data! Each object has a separate tab, which displays relevant information about that particular object.

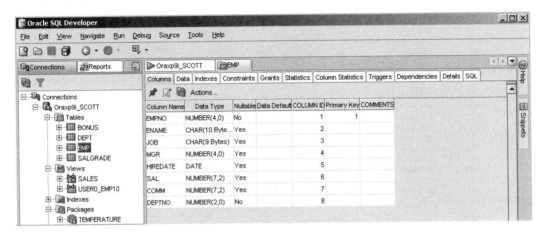

The Table Information tab display shows 11 tabs containing a variety of information about this particular table. The columns viewed here can be copied and pasted into the SQL worksheet as part of some SQL syntax. These column names can also be dragged and dropped via a mouse operation if the windows are split and the SQL worksheet is also in view. This Columns tab has four buttons: freeze view (the pin), edit, refresh, and Actions. The freeze view, when selected, does not allow SQL Developer to reuse the tab for other selections. The edit starts a wizard that allows you to modify the object, a table object in this case (i.e., add a column, drop a column, modify a column). The refresh button refreshes the display. All the tabs have an Actions button that will allow access to context-sensitive operations. The actions will differ greatly depending on the object type.

TIP
The author feels this table information is one of the most powerful features of SQL Developer. Column names can easily be copied, data can be viewed and maintained, then saved to a variety of formats (for instance, creating test data or Excel spreadsheets for users), and the table's DDL can easily be displayed (again useful for test data purposes).

The Data tab in the next image allows you to view, manipulate, and save the data displayed in a variety of formats.

	EMPNO	ENAME	JOB	MGR	HIREDATE	SAL	COMM	DEPTNO
1	7839	KING	PRESIDENT		17-NOV-00	5000		10
2	7698	BLAKE	MANAGER	7839	01-MAY-81	2850		30
3	7782	CLARK	MANAGER	7839	09-JUN-81	2450		10
4	7566	JONES	MANAGER	7839	02-APR-81	2975		20
5	7654	MARTIN	SALESMAN	7698	28-SEP-81	1250	1400	30
6	7499	ALLEN	SALESMAN	7698	20-FEB-81	1600	300	30
7	7844	TURNER	SALESMAN	7698	08-SEP-81	1500	0	30
8	7900	JAMES	CLERK	7698	03-DEC-81	950		30
9	7521	WARD	SALESMAN	7698	22-FEB-81	1250	500	30
10	7902	FORD	ANALYST	7566	03-DEC-81	3000		20
11	7369	SMITH	CLERK	7902	17-DEC-80	800		20
12	7788	SCOTT	ANALYST	7566	09-DEC-82	3000		20
13	7876	ADAMS	CLERK	7788	12-JAN-83	1100		20
14	7934	MILLER	CLERK	7782	23-JAN-82	1300		10

Notice the buttons are again context-sensitive to the type of display. Once again, the freeze view and refresh buttons are relevant to this display. When working with data, though, the + button will open a row in the data grid to insert another row. The X button will delete the row that the cursor is on. The fifth button is the commit button (writes your changes to the database), and the button to the right of this is the rollback button (does not write your changes to the database). The Sort button allows you to select columns to sort the display, and the Filter box allows you to enter a "where" clause—type in everything except for the "where" text itself. This will limit the rows returned in the display.

These changes in the data can be committed to the database. The contents of the data grid can be saved: right-click the data grid itself and Export will pop up. This Export feature is also available on the Action button. Exporting allows the displayed data to be saved in a variety of outputs as seen next. Selecting any of these options from this pop-up menu will start a wizard with specific information about the type of export operation.

The next image shows the wizard that is started. The selection from the pop-up menu is selected in the Format radio group. Select the desired output type (file or clipboard), the columns to be included (on the Columns tab), and any Where clause to only include certain rows in the output. As in the Data tab, include the where clause text but without the keyword "where."

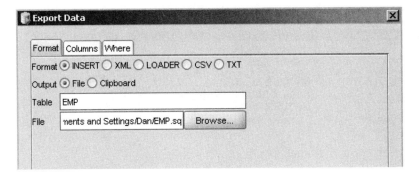

The SQL tab displays the DDL that would be useful in re-creating this table object. This type of information would be useful when building a test data script.

```
REM SCOTT EMP

  CREATE TABLE "SCOTT"."EMP"
   (    "EMPNO" NUMBER(4,0) NOT NULL ENABLE,
        "ENAME" CHAR(10 BYTE),
        "JOB" CHAR(9 BYTE),
        "MGR" NUMBER(4,0),
        "HIREDATE" DATE,
        "SAL" NUMBER(7,2),
        "COMM" NUMBER(7,2),
        "DEPTNO" NUMBER(2,0) NOT NULL ENABLE,
        CONSTRAINT "EMP_PRIMARY_KEY" PRIMARY KEY ("EMPNO") ENABLE,
        CONSTRAINT "EMP_SELF_KEY" FOREIGN KEY ("MGR")
        REFERENCES "SCOTT"."EMP" ("EMPNO") ENABLE,
        CONSTRAINT "EMP_FOREIGN_KEY" FOREIGN KEY ("DEPTNO")
        REFERENCES "SCOTT"."DEPT" ("DEPTNO") ENABLE
   ) ;
```

Executing SQL

The SQL worksheet is a nice GUI interface for working with SQL, PL/SQL blocks, and SQL scripts. SQL Developer opens a SQL worksheet once a connection is established to a database, as shown in the following image. Additional SQL worksheet windows can be opened by using the SQL Worksheet button on the toolbar, or by right-clicking a database connection and selecting Open SQL Worksheet.

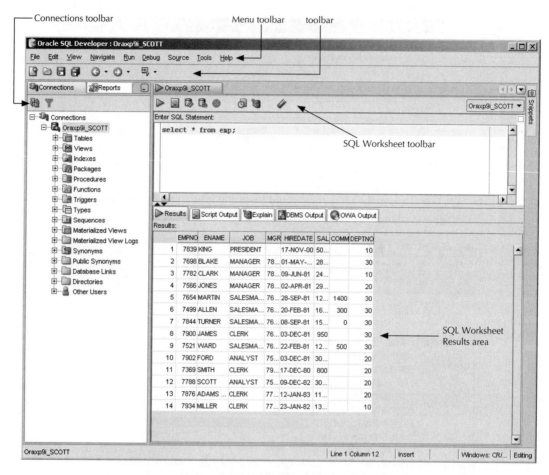

There are three ways to do just about anything in SQL Developer: by using a menu item from the Menu toolbar, by using a button on the toolbar (or a button on the specific interface toolbar), or by a predefined keystroke.

For example, you can execute a SQL statement by clicking the green arrow button (the left-most button on the SQL Worksheet toolbar) or by pressing F9. If there is more than one SQL statement in the window, make sure there is at least one blank line between the SQL statements and simply click the SQL statement you wish to execute and press F9 or the Execute Statement button on the SQL Worksheet toolbar.

The buttons on the toolbar (from left to right) are: New (for connections), Open (code from a file on the file system), Save (contents of current interface tab), Save All (saves contents of all interface tabs), back and forward buttons to walk through the available tabs, and Open SQL Worksheet (opens a new SQL Worksheet tab and prompts for the connection to associate it with).

The buttons on the SQL Worksheet toolbar (from left to right) are: Execute Statement (place the cursor on the SQL to be executed), displaying the result set in the Results output tab; Run Script (runs all SQL and SQL*Plus commands in the window), displaying the output in the Scripts Output tab; Commit; Rollback; Cancel (SQL Developer allows for canceling long-running SQL!);

▶	Execute Statement	F9
🗎	Execute Explain Plan	F6
🗎	Run Script	F5
📂	Open File	Ctrl-O
🖫	Save File	Ctrl-S
🖶	Print File	Ctrl-P
✏	Clear	Ctrl-D
⊘	Cancel	Ctrl-Q
🕑	SQL History	F8
✂	Cut	Ctrl-X
🗐	Copy	Ctrl-C
📋	Paste	Ctrl-V
	Select All	Ctrl-A
🗎	Format SQL...	Ctrl-B
	Export	▶

FIGURE 3-1. *SQL worksheet commands from a right-mouse click*

SQL History; Execute Explain Plan (populates the Explain tab in the output area); and Clear (clears the SQL worksheet).

The SQL worksheet commands are also available via a right mouse-click. Simply right-click anywhere in the SQL worksheet to also display all the command options available (see Figure 3-1).

Any PL/SQL DBMS output is displayed in the DBMS Output tab, and any PL/SQL web extension output is displayed in the OWA Output tab. Be sure to click the Set Server Output On button to see the DBMS output.

Viewing and Saving Output

The SQL worksheet has five types of output defined by the tabs under the SQL area of the interface.

The Results tab is the output from a single SQL statement execution. The image to the right shows the Results from the simple SQL statement 'select * from emp;'. The Export option seen in Figure 3-1 pertains to this output tab. You can save the output here just like the output of the Data tab from the Table Information display discussed earlier in this chapter.

Each of the other tabs has its own toolbar that will save the contents being displayed, print the contents being displayed, and clear the contents of the tab, as well as make functions available for that particular tab/feature.

▶ Results   🗎 Script Output   🗎 Explain   🗎 DBMS Output   🌐 OWA Output

Results:

	EMPNO	ENAME	JOB	MGR	HIREDATE	SAL	COMM	DEPTNO
1	7839	KING	PRESIDENT		17-NOV-00	50...		10
2	7698	BLAKE	MANAGER	78...	01-MAY-...	28...		30
3	7782	CLARK	MANAGER	78...	09-JUN-81	24...		10
4	7566	JONES	MANAGER	78...	02-APR-81	29...		20
5	7654	MARTIN	SALESMA...	76...	28-SEP-81	12...	1400	30
6	7499	ALLEN	SALESMA...	76...	20-FEB-81	16...	300	30
7	7844	TURNER	SALESMA...	76...	08-SEP-81	15...	0	30
8	7900	JAMES	CLERK	76...	03-DEC-81	950		30
9	7521	WARD	SALESMA...	76...	22-FEB-81	12...	500	30
10	7902	FORD	ANALYST	75...	03-DEC-81	30...		20
11	7369	SMITH	CLERK	79...	17-DEC-80	800		20
12	7788	SCOTT	ANALYST	75...	09-DEC-82	30...		20
13	7876	ADAMS ...	CLERK	77...	12-JAN-83	11...		20
14	7934	MILLER	CLERK	77...	23-JAN-82	13...		10

The Script Output tab displays the results when the Run Script button is pressed.

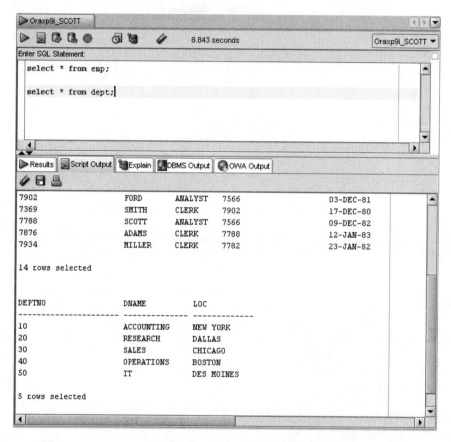

SQL Developer can run an explain plan for the selected SQL statement in the SQL area. Simply click the Explain Plan button on the SQL Worksheet toolbar or press F6 to see the explain plan.

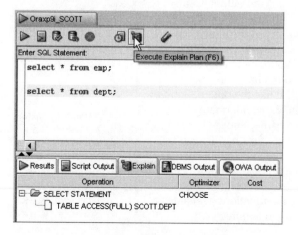

The DBMS Output tab displays any DBMS output from any PL/SQL that was executed in the SQL worksheet. Notice this tab has its own specific toolbar. The left-most button enables DBMS output. The next three buttons are clear, save, and print. The DBMS output buffer size is adjustable, as is the rate of time that SQL Developer will poll the DBMS output area for additional output.

Working with SQL

SQL Developer allows you to enter SQL, open files that contain SQL and SQL scripts, or create SQL from templates. SQL Developer can easily create a SELECT statement completely set up for any table. Simply drag and drop a table name from the Connections Navigator tables item and drop it into the SQL worksheet. Figure 3-2 shows the SQL statement that is automatically generated for you.

SQL Developer will allow SQL to be pasted in, opened (using File | Open, the toolbar open button, or CTRL-O), or double-clicked from the file system. When SQL Developer is executed for the first time, SQL Developer will prompt you to associate all .SQL files with SQL Developer. If you select Yes, then double-clicking SQL files using the Windows Explorer (on a PC, for example) will start SQL Developer, open a SQL worksheet, and put the contents of the file into the SQL Worksheet window.

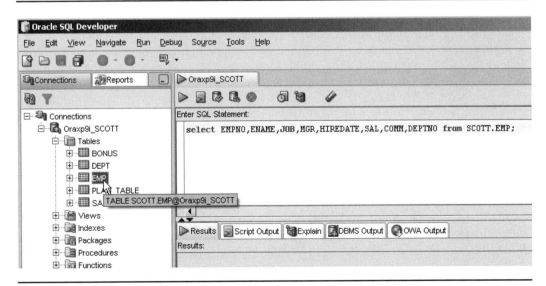

FIGURE 3-2. *Automatic SQL statement generation*

Coding Assistants

There are several coding assistants available in SQL Developer. The first method is code snippets: code templates, pieces of code, and optimizer hints that can be added to your SQL code via a drag-and-drop operation. The next is code insights. Code insights display pop-up boxes with information about either columns or procedure/function options. Code insights are triggered by typing a period (.). The other code assistant available is code completion insights. This assistant displays available packages and is triggered by CTRL-SPACE.

Snippets are pieces of code, code templates, and hints useful in developing SQL and PL/SQL, and in tuning SQL statements. Snippets are accessed via the View menu.

Code snippets gives instant access to a variety of useful information. These code templates, pieces of code, conversion functions, mathematical functions, and optimizer hints are simply put into the SQL code via a drag-and-drop operation. This snippet interface also includes PL/SQL code examples and pseudo-columns.

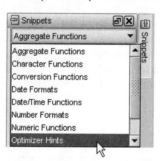

The next image shows an optimizer hint being added to the generic SQL statement from Figure 3-2. Simply hover the mouse over any snippet in this interface for a description of what it can do.

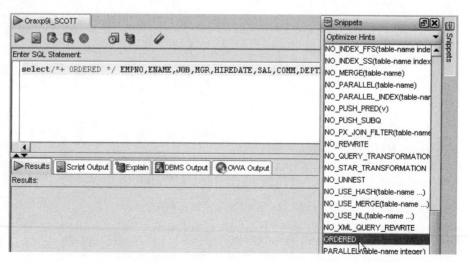

The snippet window can "autohide." Click the "-" in the upper-right corner of the snippet window to move it to the other side of the SQL Developer interface, or right-click it and select Float to undock it from the SQL Developer interface.

Code insights are useful to display table columns in a pop-up menu selection or available Oracle package options, again, in a pop-up menu selection. Both types of selections are triggered by entering the table name or the package name followed by a period (.) and simply waiting a second. The image on the left shows the available columns for the EMP table, and the image on the right shows the available package options for the package DBMS_OUTPUT. Click an entry and hit ENTER or double-click a column to make your selection.

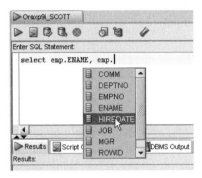 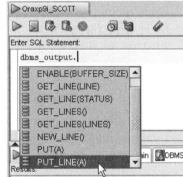

The code completion insights feature gives a list of available package names. Simply press CTRL-SPACE and a pop-up menu of all available Oracle packages will appear. Scroll through the list to find the package desired. To get the options for these packages, simply press CTRL-SPACE again or use the "." after the package name as with code insights.

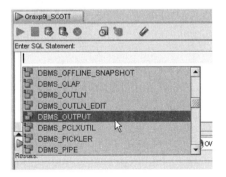

Using Code Templates

The snippets panel has PL/SQL Programming Techniques templates. There are many code examples in these templates. Simply drag and drop the code example you desire into the SQL worksheet or the PL/SQL Code Editor. The next image illustrates the IF-THEN-ELSEIF template in use.

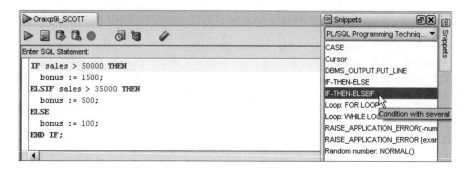

Using SQL History

SQL History is a nice feature that saves the SQL executed (using the Execute Statement button or F9) in the SQL worksheet for future reference. SQL History is accessed by using the F8 key, or by clicking the SQL History button on the SQL Worksheet toolbar. The next image shows the SQL History interface. To retrieve SQL, simply click it and select Replace (to clear the SQL worksheet and add the SQL) or Append (to add the SQL at the end of the existing code in the SQL worksheet). The Clear button empties the SQL history. There is a filter option to help find the SQL statement with specific strings (such as a table name, perhaps). Any of the columns can be sorted in ascending or descending order by clicking the column heading.

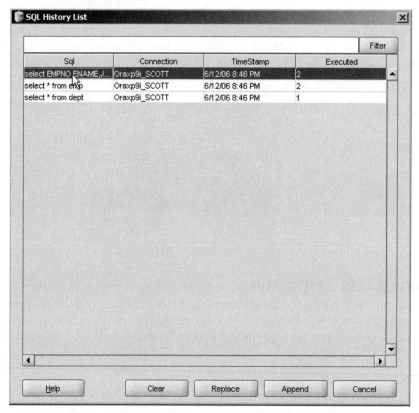

Executing SQL Scripts

SQL Developer allows you to execute more than one SQL statement at a time, or to run SQL*Plus scripts. These scripts can include PL/SQL blocks and SQL*Plus commands. As seen next, the SQL*Plus commands are noted but not executed. Not all SQL*Plus commands are supported. To execute the contents of the SQL worksheet as a script, press F5 or click the Execute Script button on the SQL worksheet toolbar. Use this button to execute more than one SQL statement or function at the same time. The output is displayed in the SQL Script output tab.

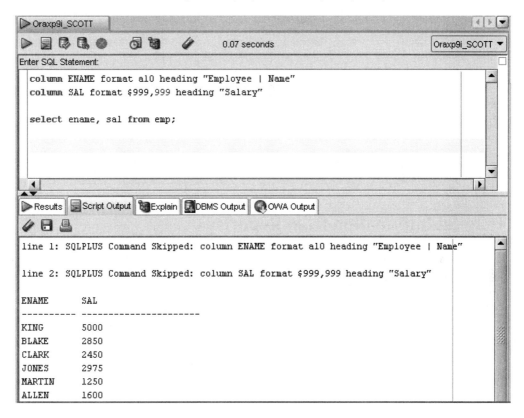

Executing PL/SQL

PL/SQL code can be executed through the SQL worksheet with the F9 key or Execute command. Any DBMS_OUTPUT will be displayed in the DBMS_OUTPUT tab. PL/SQL functions are included in the text of the SQL statement or by variable assignment in PL/SQL. The next image shows the execution and output of a simple PL/SQL block. Make sure to enable DBMS output by clicking the left-most button on the DBMS Output tab toolbar.

Useful Information from Reports

SQL Developer has a host of useful reports available on the Reports Navigation interface. The first time a report is executed, SQL Developer will prompt for an available connection and then execute the report against data in the connected Oracle database.

Many reports will prompt for a bind variable. For example, the Free Space report will prompt for a tablespace name. If this value is left null, all free space for all tablespaces for the Oracle instance the connection is connected to will be displayed.

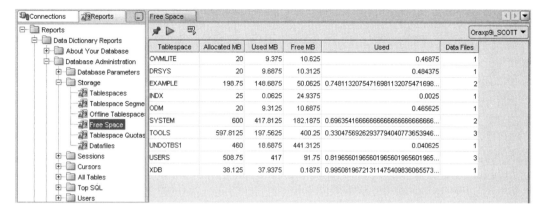

Tablespace	Allocated MB	Used MB	Free MB	Used	Data Files
CWMLITE	20	9.375	10.625	0.46875	1
DRSYS	20	9.6875	10.3125	0.484375	1
EXAMPLE	198.75	148.6875	50.0625	0.7481132075471698113207547169...	2
INDX	25	0.0625	24.9375	0.0025	1
ODM	20	9.3125	10.6875	0.465625	1
SYSTEM	600	417.8125	182.1875	0.6963541666666666666666666666...	2
TOOLS	597.8125	197.5625	400.25	0.3304756926293779404077365394...	3
UNDOTBS1	460	18.6875	441.3125	0.040625	1
USERS	508.75	417	91.75	0.8196560196560196560196560196...	3
XDB	38.125	37.9375	0.1875	0.9950819672131147540983606557...	1

Notice the buttons on the report toolbar. The red pin will "freeze," or pin, this information so that this report and its contents are preserved when running additional reports (otherwise, SQL Developer will reuse the same tab for the next report selected). The Execute button will rerun the report. The SQL Worksheet button will put the SQL that generated this report into the SQL worksheet. This is a useful learning tool to discover where Oracle saves useful information. This SQL is also available for modifications, and you can then add this new SQL to a user-defined report. Simply right-click User Defined Reports to add folders and SQL for your own reports.

There are ten major categories for Reports. The contents of each of these reports will be covered in Chapter 9.

Summary

The goal of this chapter is to survey the major features of SQL Developer. The idea here is to give you enough information to be productive with this tool and give you a working knowledge of several of its useful interfaces and code assistants. Topics covered include navigating around the SQL Developer interfaces, displaying and changing data, saving data, working with SQL (and its various templates and code assistants), and illustrating the Reports interface. These features should easily get you productive with SQL Developer.

PART

II

Using SQL Developer

CHAPTER
4

General Information

his section will cover general features of the SQL Developer window interface.

The SQL Developer appearance and assistants are very adjustable to the user's personal preference and degree of expertise with the tool. Toolbars can be removed; window interfaces can be closed, undocked (allowed to float around on the screen), split, combined, and closed.

SQL Developer allows for several windows to undock from the tool itself, allowing the user to move undocked windows to convenient locations about the screen. SQL Developer will reuse the tabs when other object display information is selected. Pinning tabs (using the freeze or pushpin button on the tab's toolbar) allows for useful information to remain available while other information is being selected. Tab groups allow for the selected active tab displays to be visible at the same time. This chapter will also detail the preferences and options of SQL Developer.

Viewing and Hiding Toolbars

The SQL Developer main toolbar and the toolbar on the Connections tab can be easily turned on and off via the Menu | View | Toolbars menu items. The next image shows how these toolbars are displayed or hidden from display, or redisplayed if hidden.

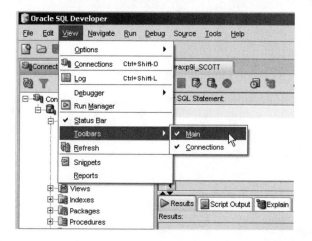

Opening and Closing Interfaces

The SQL Developer displays all have the ability to be opened, maximized, minimized, or closed. This image illustrates that when the mouse is hovered over the tab on any tabbed display, an X to close the display will appear. The keystroke combination SHIFT-ESC will also close the active tab.

Use a right-click to display the context menu options for that tab.

These are the Tab Display options:

- Move allows moving the tabbed display to another part of the SQL Developer display.
- Size will allow the display to be resized.
- Float allows the display to be undocked (see "Dockable Windows" later in this chapter).
- Minimize will shrink the display and put an icon along the outer edge of the display. This display becomes an autohide-type display as is discussed later in this chapter. As long as it is minimized, it can be accessed by moving the mouse near it; the display will reopen while the mouse is in the display.
- Maximize will return the display to a static and open status.
- Close will close the display.

Notice next that when any interface is selected, the title bar of SQL Developer will reflect the interface and the database connection associated with the interface. Hovering the mouse over the tab of the interface will pop up the same information.

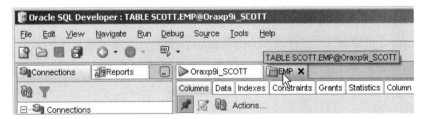

The SQL worksheet can be opened by clicking the SQL Worksheet button on the toolbar. This option will prompt for a connection to be selected. Clicking the down arrow right next to the SQL Worksheet button will display the established connections in SQL Developer and allow the user to open the SQL worksheet using an existing connection to the database. SQL worksheet interfaces can also be opened from the SQL Developer menu bar option Tools | SQL Worksheet menu selection.

SQL Developer interfaces and displays are accessed via various methods. The table or any database object display interface is opened from the Connections Navigator under the respective object node. Simply click one of the object names to open a tab and display a variety of information relevant to the object you selected.

The Connections/Reports Navigator interface can also be opened and closed as desired using SQL Developer menu bar option View and selecting either the Connections or the Reports item.

The SQL Developer Object displays are accessed by opening the object type and clicking the object type name. The next image illustrates the EMP table object appearing in a tab display.

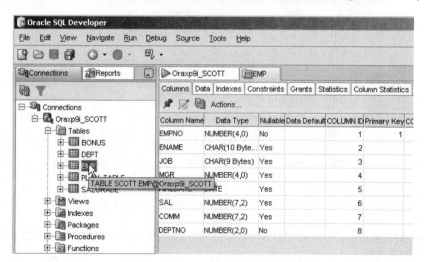

PL/SQL objects have the same toolbar and tabbed interfaces as the other objects. The next image shows a simple procedure being opened with a mouse-click operation. Click the second button (Edit) on the tab's toolbar to load this code into the PL/SQL Code Editor interface window for editing.

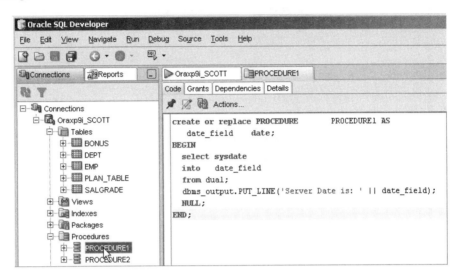

The object tabbed display interfaces are also controlled with a right-click pop-up menu operation. The tab can be maximized (to the entire SQL Developer interface), split or grouped (as discussed in the next section of this chapter), or closed. The Close All option closes all the object and SQL Worksheet interfaces; Close Others closes all the other interfaces and SQL worksheets except for the selected one (i.e., the one right-clicked on).

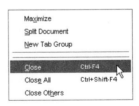

TIP
Double-click a tab to maximize it and double-click again to return to the previous size.

Customizing the Display

SQL Developer allows for any of the displayed navigators, snippets, help, and interface displays to be relocated to any position desired. This behavior might be desirable to be able to see both the SQL worksheet and one or more table displays. Simply click and drag the tab to the desired location. A blue transparent box will appear that will indicate the new position of the display if the mouse is released. Keep moving the mouse around the display until the desired position is visualized.

Let go of the mouse button and the display will be repositioned. The next image shows the EMP table display split away from the SQL worksheet, allowing the user to now drag and drop column names from the EMP table display onto the SQL worksheet.

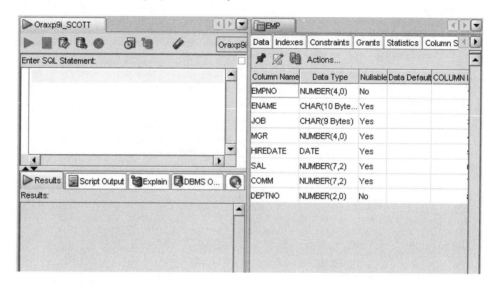

Any number of displayed tabs can be relocated around the SQL Developer display. When SQL Developer is closed, these tab/interface displays are remembered, and the new look of SQL Developer is reestablished the next time SQL Developer is started.

Returning the split tabs to a single tabbed display is accomplished in one of two ways. Click the tab and drag it until a blue transparent location box appears inside the original location and release the mouse button, or right-click the tab and select Collapse Tab Groups. This operation will return the moved tabs back to their original locations.

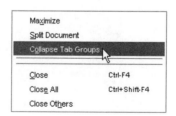

Dockable Windows

The Snippets, Help, and Connections/Report Navigator windows are all undockable, or allowed to float around the display screen with a mouse drag-and-drop operation. To undock any of these windows, right-click the tab of the display desired to be undocked. Select Float from the pop-up menu.

TIP
These windows can also be undocked and docked with drag-and-drop operations.

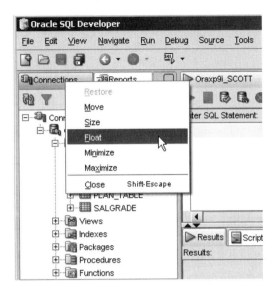

The window is now undocked and can be moved to any location of the display. Items in the window can still be dragged and dropped into other SQL Developer interface screens.

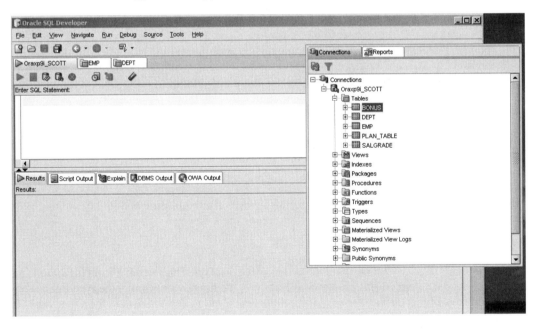

To re-dock the windows to their prior location, right-click the tab of the display desired to be docked and select Dock, as shown in the next image. This operation will return the display to its prior location in SQL Developer prior to undocking.

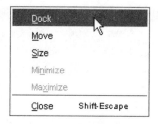

Pinning Displays

The object display interfaces have the ability to pin or "freeze" the view or data they are displaying. When the red pushpin is clicked, SQL Developer will open a new tab for a new display selection rather than reuse a tab that is already open from a prior object display selection. SQL Developer will reuse existing tabs by default if the tab is not pinned. This image shows the Freeze View button as well as what happens when the Dept table item is clicked with the EMP table display already open and pinned.

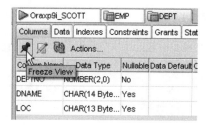

Autohide Displays

The Connections and Report Navigators, Snippets, Help system, and debugger tabs can each be set to minimize to an icon along the outside of the SQL Developer interface. When the mouse pointer is near the icon, the navigator or assistant interface that is minimized will pop open to its original size, and when the mouse pointer is moved away from the specific interface, the box will return to its minimized state as an icon. To minimize, click the "-" button on the interface header or right-click the tab and select Minimize. To maximize, or stop the autohide feature, click the restore button next on the interface header itself or right-click and select Maximize. The Snippets and Help interfaces in their minimized, or autohidden, state are shown here.

TIP

The minimized or autohidden tabs can be moved to either side of SQL Developer by simply dragging and dropping the icon.

Splitting Tab Displays

The object displays can be split into two or more displays. This feature allows for various types of data per data object display to be visible at the same time. For example, the next image shows the EMP table object display showing the column information and the data in the same view. To split an object display, right-click and select Split Document.

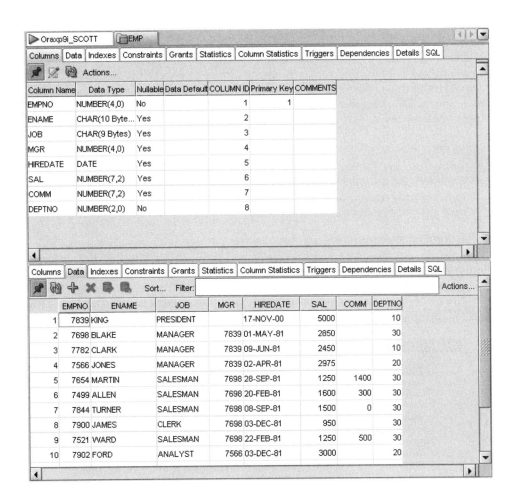

TIP
Splitting tab windows can also be accomplished by a drag-and-drop operation. Click and hold on the tab and move it around the screen to split or even undock the window. SQL Developer will show blue highlights to where the screen will be split or undocked as the mouse is moved.

The next image shows this menu item. If another split display is desired, repeat the process. To collapse the displays, right-click and select Unsplit Document.

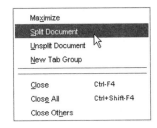

Maximize	
Split Document	
Unsplit Document	
New Tab Group	
Close	Ctrl-F4
Close All	Ctrl+Shift-F4
Close Others	

TIP
Using the menus to split the tabs will only allow for horizontal groupings of the tabs. Using the drag-and-drop method, tabs can be grouped vertically as well.

Preferences

SQL Developer has preferences that control and maintain the desired default behavior. There are 12 major categories for preferences. This section will discuss each and the effects each has on the SQL Developer environment. To access the Preferences interface, select the menu item Tools | Preferences.

NOTE
When installing a newer version of SQL Developer, you will be prompted "do you want to migrate . . . ." Answering yes to this question will preserve these settings. If you delete SQL Developer and then install the newer version, these settings will be lost.

Environment Preferences

The environment preferences drive the default behavior, such as saving unsaved changes to the file system or saving changes before compiling. Many of these options are self-explanatory. The look and feel give SQL Developer a different window appearance. The Theme changes the color scheme.

The Environment has three sub-categories that control if windows are dockable, how much local history to save (changes to files), and how to save the contents of the log files.

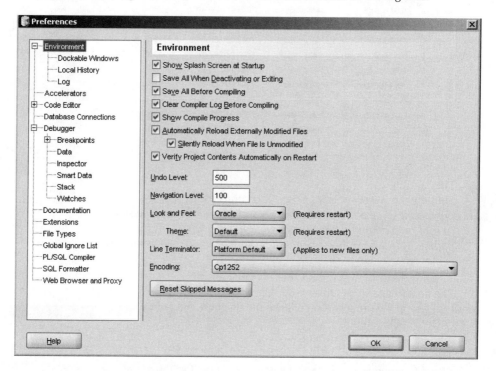

NOTE
The help button in the lower left of each of these preferences screens will give specific information about the options visible.

The SQL History file is stored in the documents and settings folder under .sqldeveloper (on a PC) and is not interrupted with SQL Developer upgrades.

Accelerators Preferences

SQL Developer has literally dozens of hot keys or accelerator keystrokes. These key sequences activate different features of SQL Developer without your having to leave the keyboard and do a mouse operation. They include several industry-standard key sequences such as CTRL-C for copy, CTRL-V for paste, CTRL-O for open, and CTRL-S for save.

This interface shows all of the key sequences assigned to tasks in SQL Developer. These key sequences, or accelerators, can be removed by highlighting the accelerator and clicking Remove. New accelerators can be added by filling in the New Accelerator and the key sequence and clicking OK. The next image shows the key sequence for the Clear accelerator. Notice the Load Preset button on the lower-right corner of the interface. This will restore all of the accelerators to their original settings.

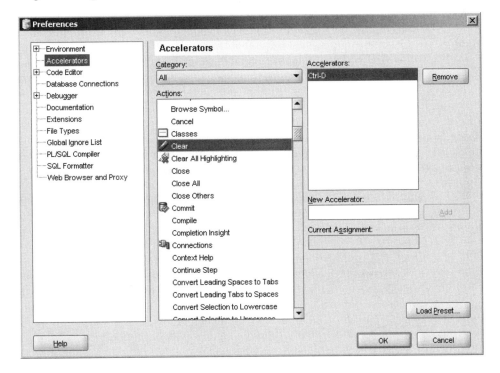

Code Editor Preferences

The PL/SQL code editor is used to edit procedures, functions, and packages and has eleven subcategories of preferences. These preferences control everything from cursor appearance, bookmarking, and colors/fonts to word wrapping. The main PL/SQL code editor preferences allow for default line and word handling.

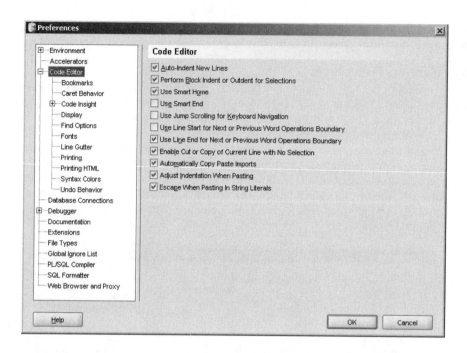

Code Editor Bookmark Preferences   Bookmarks are a useful aid to quickly jump around to portions of code of interest in code modules that are rather large in size. The Bookmark Preferences regulate how and when SQL Developer saves bookmarks placed in code modules.

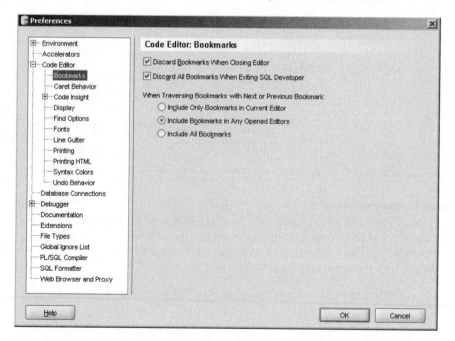

Caret Behavior Preferences   Caret behavior allows for the color, shape, and activity of the cursor in the PL/SQL code editor and SQL Worksheet to be changed. There are eight different shapes for the insert mode and overwrite mode of the cursor.

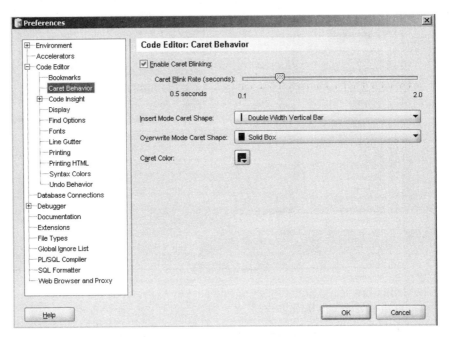

Code Insight Preferences   Code insights are pop-ups in the SQL worksheet and PL/SQL code editor interfaces that will display object information as you type in the interface. The next image shows that the font and size of the text in the pop-up can be controlled, as can how much time is required to activate the pop-up.

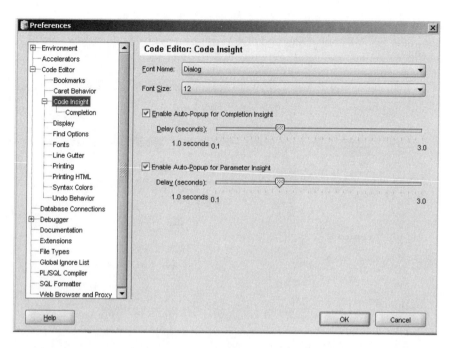

The Code Completion preference is a subcategory to the Code Insights. The type of information displayed can be adjusted.

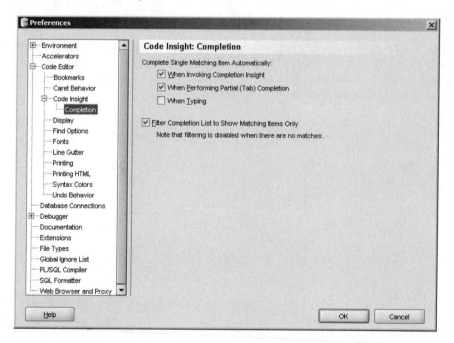

Any of these automatic assistants can be completely turned off.

TIP
*If SQL Developer is taking too long to function on larger files, it might
be the code insight and completion assistants slowing you down.*

Code Editor Display Preferences   This preference screen allows for adjustments to the display
attributes of the PL/SQL code editor. Notice the last option shown controls the delay when typing
(, [, or { before SQL Developer will check for the matching parenthesis, brace, or bracket.

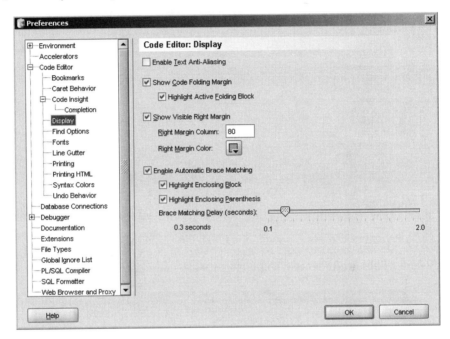

Code Editor Find Options Preferences   This preference interface allows for specific default
behavior when doing word or phrase searches in any text. This preference also allows SQL
Developer to remember the prior search string from the last time SQL Developer had been started.

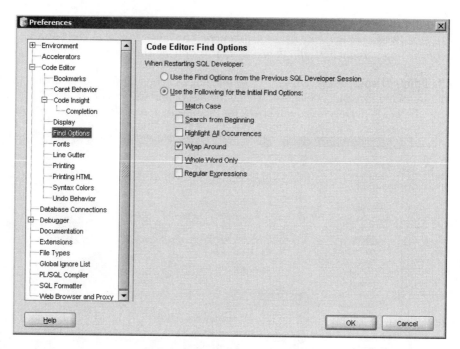

Multiple options can be selected in the Initial Find Options area.

Code Editor Font Preferences   This preference allows the default text font and size to be selected.

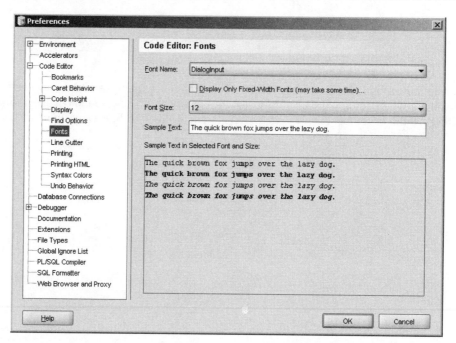

Code Editor Line Gutter Preferences   The line gutters control the area around the text entry area of the PL/SQL code editor. The highlight here, besides being able to change the colors of the gutters, is the ability to add code line numbers.

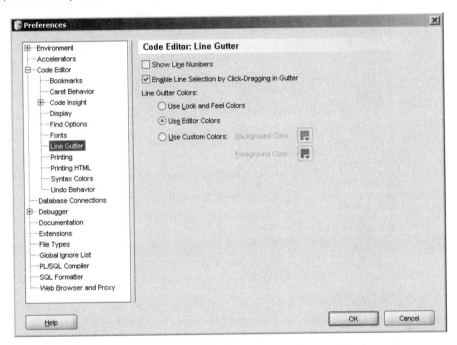

NOTE
You can display line numbers at any time while using the PL/SQL code editor by using the context menu and selecting Toggle Line Numbers (i.e., right-click the gutter to access the context menu).

Code Editor Printing Preferences   SQL Developer can print the contents of the PL/SQL code editor with a different font and font size than that assigned to the PL/SQL code editor itself. Other useful options include the ability to print line numbers, page numbers, and header information (name of the code, etc), as well as choose whether to wrap long lines.

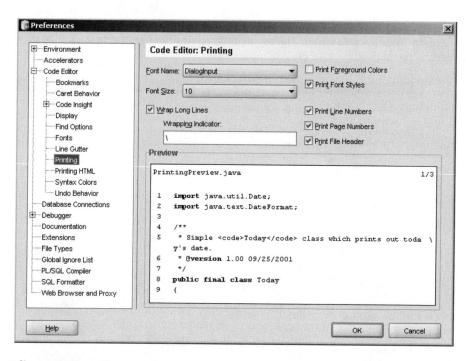

Code Editor Printing HTML Preferences   These preferences are similar to the printing options but apply to the HTML output being printed from SQL Developer.

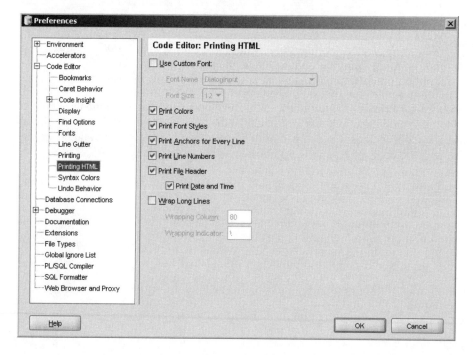

Code Editor Syntax Colors Preferences   SQL Developer allows for any feature of the syntax in the PL/SQL code editor to be changed, bolded, highlighted, etc. The next image illustrates the options available to control the appearance of the syntax as it is entered and displayed in the PL/SQL code editor. Notice at the bottom under Scheme that several color schemes are available for the syntax, and that any change made can be saved to an existing color scheme or to a new color scheme (using the Save As button).

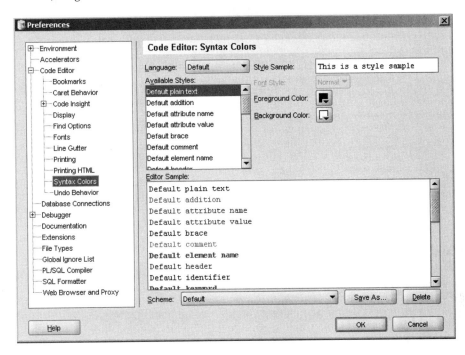

Undo Behavior   This preference controls the undo behavior of the PL/SQL code editor. Notice that undo can be grouped together to undo several changes at a time.

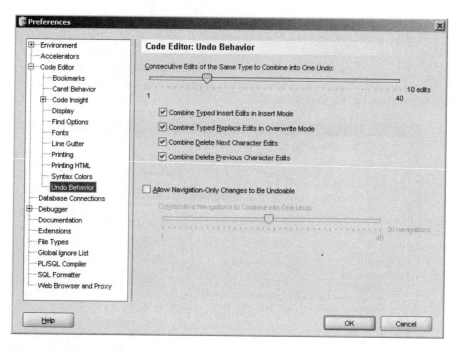

Database Connections Preferences

The database connections preferences include the autocommit feature for the SQL worksheet, defining the SQL*Plus tool location.

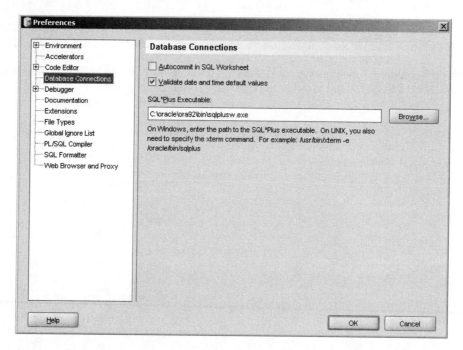

Debugger Preferences

The PL/SQL code editor's debugger options are easy to adjust. Notice that the debugger toolbar can be disabled; the behavior of the debugger itself can be adjusted as well (note the Start Debugging Option group).

The debugger has specific subcategories for each part of the debugger.

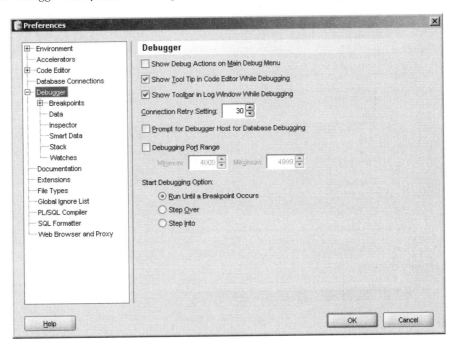

Debugger Breakpoints Preferences   The debugger breakpoint initialization points can be adjusted. Multiple column attributes can be selected for breakpoints. The scope of using the breakpoints can be set across SQL Developer.

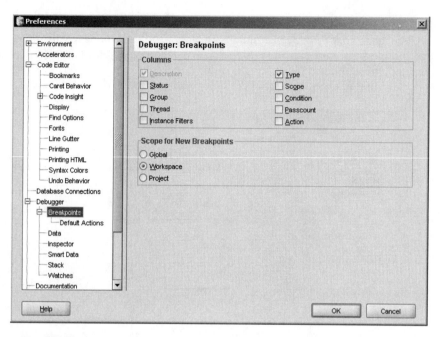

The breakpoint preferences include a subcategory that controls the behavior when a breakpoint occurs.

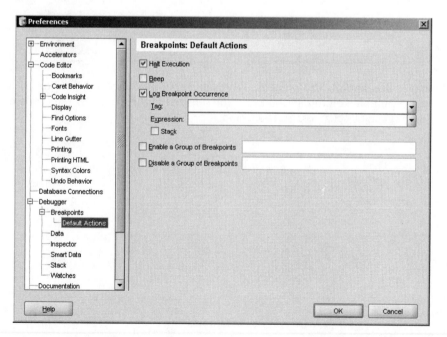

Debugger Data Preferences   Several options control how the data appears (multiple display types of data can be selected), the order of the displayed columns, and the way to display null values.

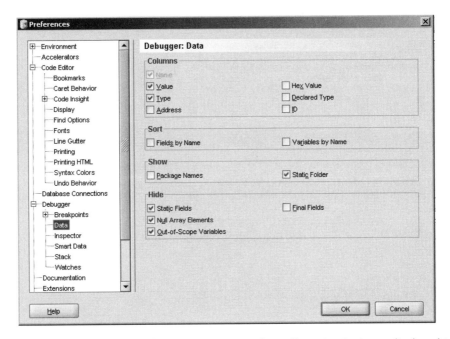

Debugger Inspector Display Preferences   This interface allows for the items displayed in the Inspector output area to be adjusted.

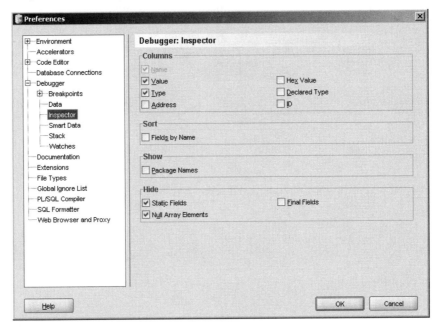

Debugger Smart Data Display Preferences   This preference interface allows for the adjustment of the items and how they appear in the Smart Data display of the debugger.

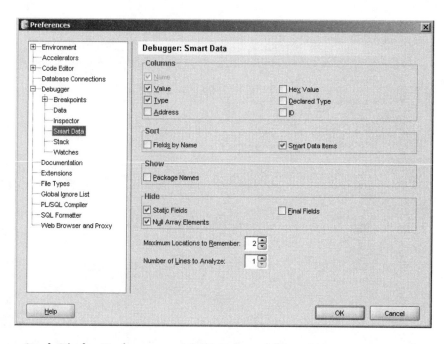

Debugger Stack Display Preferences   SQL Developer allows for specific or additional information to be displayed in the call stack window of the debugger. The next image shows all available options. Additional output options are simply checked.

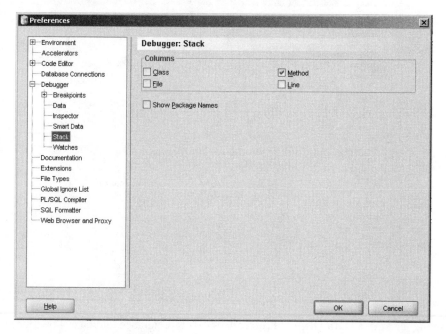

Debugger Watch Display Preferences   The watch display can be adjusted as well. Notice the available options.

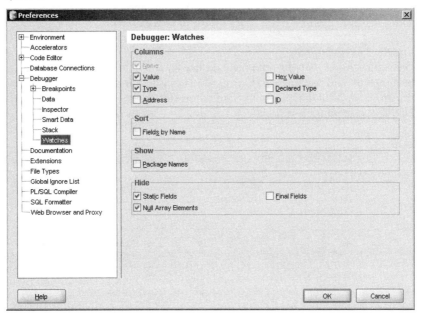

Documentation Preferences

This documentation item is part of the SQL Developer Help environment. This part refers to the online help. Checking the Display In Window box will display the online help in its own window.

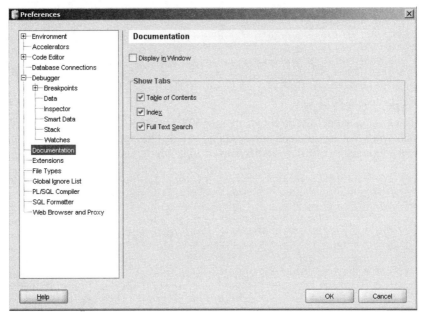

TIP
Displaying help in its own window is very useful if you have a large monitor or even dual monitors for display. You can move the help onto a separate monitor or off to the side and continue working.

Extensions Preferences

This preference works with the automatic update feature of SQL Developer. This automatic feature can be turned off and the ability to look for updates is in this preference. Extensions can be used to add functionality to SQL Developer. This screen allows for no, some, or all extensions to be included. Checking this on will allow for automatic updates of certain extensions. Check this off, and the user will have to check for updates manually.

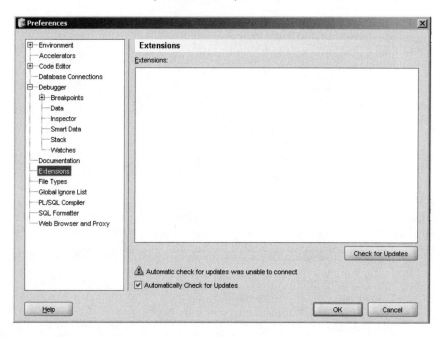

File Types Preferences

The file types preferences control two areas of SQL Developer. The File Types tab shows the various file suffix types that are automatically assigned to SQL Developer. The Default Editors tab shows the different editor assignments to various parts of SQL Developer.

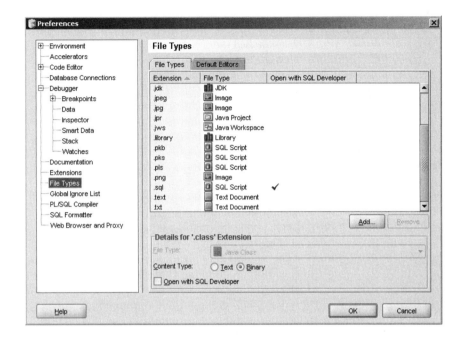

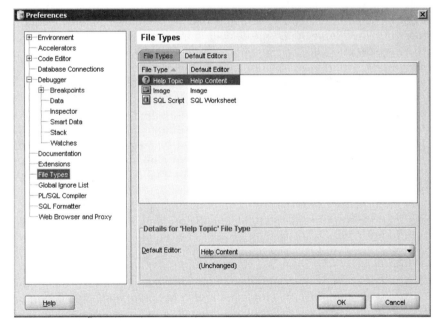

Global Ignore List Preferences

The global ignore list is the opposite of the file types mentioned in the prior section. If a file type is listed here, SQL Developer will not include it in any processing.

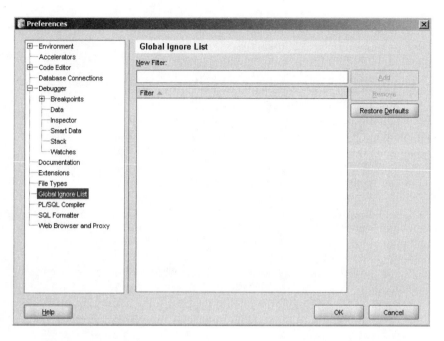

PL/SQL Compiler Preferences

The PL/SQL compiler preferences are used to override the Oracle RDBMS defaults. Leaving these selections blank will leave the Oracle defaults in effect. Each category has Enable, Disable, or Error message display options.

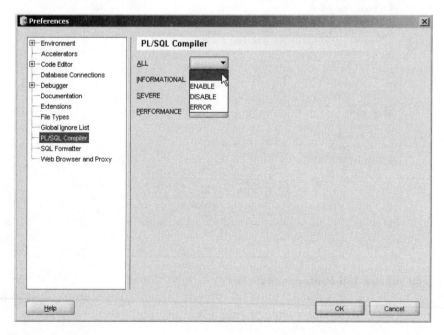

SQL Formatter Preferences

These SQL Formatter options give control over how SQL will be formatted when this option is selected in the SQL Worksheet interface.

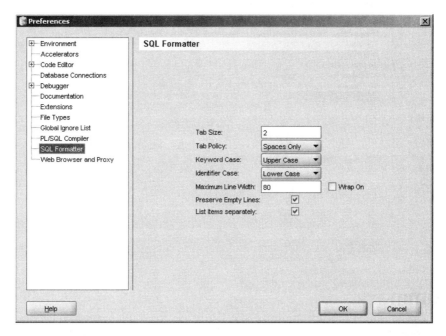

Web Browser and Proxy

These preferences allow SQL Developer to run the web browser on your computer system and to access the Internet using your network credentials. The next image shows specific required details when using the web interfaces associated with SQL Developer.

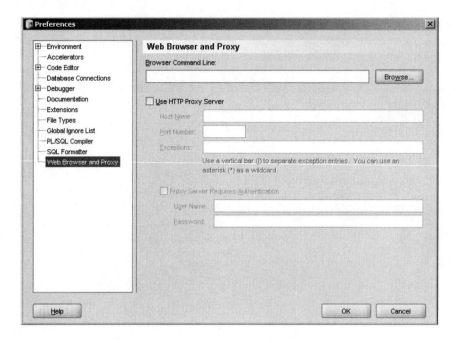

Summary

This chapter shows how to customize SQL Developer for your personal preferences. SQL Developer allows for all of the interfaces to be moved about, and many of the interfaces can be undocked so that they can be located to a more convenient location on the screen. Several of the interfaces have an autohide feature when minimized so that they appear when needed and stay hidden when not but are quickly and easily accessed.

CHAPTER
5

Working with the
Connections Navigator

Working with Objects

his chapter focuses on the database objects on the Connections Navigator window. Topics such as refreshing connections, filtering objects, connection maintenance, and starting or maintaining any of the supported database objects are covered in detail. The accompanying image shows the Connections Navigator window and the available SCOTT user database objects.

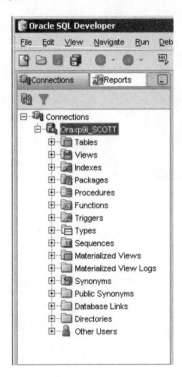

NOTE
SQL Developer does not allow you to perform any task that you do not have database privileges to perform.

The Connections Navigator Toolbar

The Connections Navigator is SQL Developer's main interface to accessing and creating database objects. The various SQL Developer definition interfaces are also automatically selected, depending on the context of the object being accessed. For example, when accessing the table or view navigator items, a tab is opened in the SQL Worksheet window that displays column names, data, and other information about these object types. Each of the database objects displays information about the particular object selected, and each will be discussed later in this chapter. The Procedures, Packages, and Functions tab shows object details in the SQL Worksheet window with their definitions displayed in tabs in the same way as the other database objects. You can review the code in one of the tabs and invoke a separate PL/SQL Code Interface tab for editing and debugging the code.

TIP
In most cases, you should be able to learn useful SQL syntax by viewing the SQL that SQL Developer has created to meet your request.

Refreshing Connections

The first button, the double arrows, is the connection refresh. It will become available when a connection on this navigator window is selected. The refresh will have SQL Developer close the existing connection, reopen it, and open a fresh SQL Worksheet window.

Filtering Database Objects

The second button, filter, is active when a database object type is selected under the Database Connection. This button is context-sensitive to the database item selected and allows for a filtering operation to be performed on the available items under the particular database item. A right-click operation on these database items will also allow for filtering the displayed objects.

Select the Tables object and click the Filter button to open the Filter Objects dialog box. Using syntax from the SQL "LIKE" command, only table objects that meet the pattern in the dialog box will be displayed. The image shows the dialog box being filled out to search for objects with names that start with a "D"; the "%" is the global character that tells SQL Developer to include any number of characters after the "D".

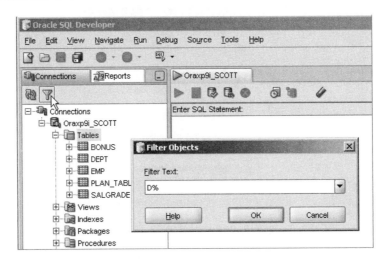

The next image on the left shows the results of the filtering. Notice that the filtering criterion also appears in the database object field. To remove the filter, either click the Apply Filter button on the Connections Navigator toolbar and return the search criterion to a "%", or right-click the database object being filtered and select Clear Filter from the context menu as illustrated on the right.

Working with Connections

Getting connected to the database is easy with SQL Developer. Chapter 2 covered setting up and maintaining database connections. To get connected, simply click the "+" or right-click the Connections item and select Connect from the context menu. A connection is not required to view SQL from the computer's file system, view reports, and view snippets. SQL Developer will prompt for a database connection when a database operation is requested (such as when it is asked to execute the SQL from a file or to run a selected report).

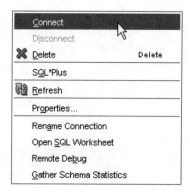

You can do these additional things from the Database Connection context menu:

- Close (disconnect), delete, or refresh the database connection.
- Start SQL*Plus. Since SQL Developer is far more robust with its connection options than SQL*Plus, however, login and connection information will need to be provided when SQL*Plus prompts for it. The SQL*Plus executable location will have to be set up in the Database Connections preferences discussed in Chapter 4. The Properties selection will allow for the connection information to be displayed and changed, as discussed in Chapter 2.

■   Rename the connection (note that all windows associated with the connection will be closed).

■   Open additional SQL Worksheet windows.

■   Enable Remote Debug.

■   Gather cost-based optimizer statistics for all objects owned by this user. This statistics-collection option has an optional percentage used to estimate statistics, and the SQL statement being executed can be viewed.

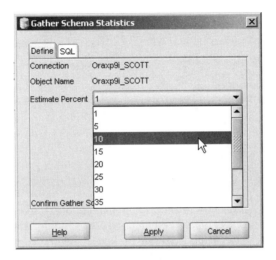

 NOTE
The Gather Schema Statistics dialog box will use the package
DBMS_STATS to collect statistics on all relevant objects owned by this
schema. Each of the relevant data objects (such as tables and indexes)
will allow for statistics to be collected on just that single object.

Opening and Closing Objects

Click the "+" in the Connections Navigator tree display to open a selected database object and see the objects below; click the "–" to close the selected database object display.

Each database object has a context menu (right-click the object) that allows for control over the filtering of displayed items under this database object and starts a wizard for creating a new object of the type selected.

Click a database object name under the Connections Navigator to open a tab in the main SQL Developer interface and view context-sensitive information across a series of tabs in the SQL

Worksheet window. The next image shows the available indexes for this database connection. Each object type has useful information along with useful DDL in the SQL tab for reference or perhaps to save for a test script.

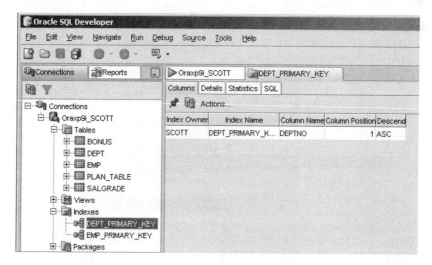

Each object type has a series of actions that can perform a series of actions specific to that object type. These actions are available from both from the object information display (see the toolbar in the preceding image) and from a right-click on the object name in the Connections Navigator, as shown here.

Working with Database Objects

The database objects are displayed in Connections Navigator window. Each option will allow for filtering, clearing filters, and refreshing the list of displayed objects for that object type. Invoke the context menu (right-click the database object name) for the database object to access the database object high-level options shown next. Most options allow access to a dialog box that will assist in creating a new object of that type. This section covers each option in these "Create" object dialog boxes for each of these database objects.

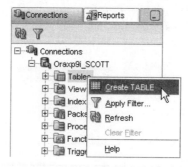

Create Table Object

Tables are the main data storage structure in Oracle. The next image shows the Create Table dialog box. This display shows the variables required to make a table object with a minimum of effort. Notice the Add Column and Remove Column buttons at the bottom of the screen. Also notice the DDL tab, which will show the SQL syntax as columns and syntax are added in the Columns tab.

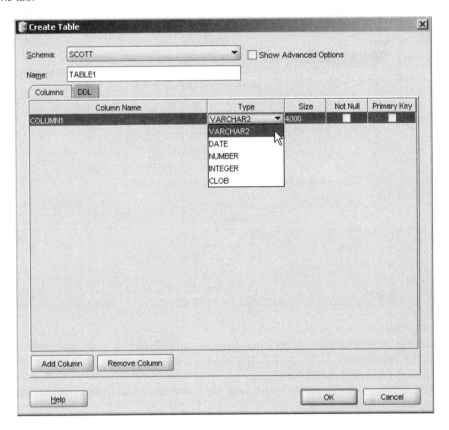

If you click OK, this object will be created in the connected user's database schema using all defaults assigned to the user (for tablespace parameters) and will use the default storage clause assigned to the user's default tablespace.

The image on the next page shows the Advanced options accessed by clicking the Show Advanced Options box. This dialog box gives the user total control over the creation of every aspect of the table object. Once the table is created, these definitions can be viewed and most can be changed. For example, if partitioning is not defined when creating the table, then this option will not appear when editing the table definitions later. Notice the Add and Remove column buttons have been replaced with a "+" and "–" and that there is a feature under these buttons to move the column location within the display of columns.

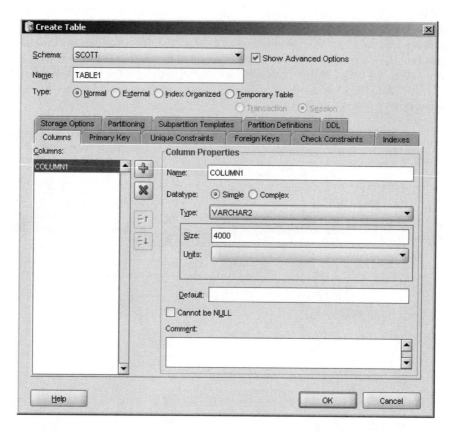

There are tabs on this display to add or remove a variety of constraints (primary key, unique constraints, foreign keys, and check constraints), add indexes, tailor storage options, and work with a variety of partitioning options. There is still a DDL tab to see the syntax of the Create Table syntax as built by this dialog box.

A radio group just under the table name allows various table types to be included in the syntax and resulting database table object.

NOTE
Consult the Database SQL Reference Guide for specific details on any of these syntax options.

Working with Table Objects

Each database object in the Connections Navigator will display information, and the data-oriented objects will display data and allow the data to be maintained. The next image shows the Table Display information window. Notice the tab title contains the EMP table object name. Chapter 4 showed how to split this window, freeze this window, and refresh this window. The toolbar just under the tabs is also context sensitive. Most of the object display information windows will have the pin, refresh, and actions buttons. Most of the database objects allow for editing (using the edit button), but some objects, such as Indexes, don't allow for updates, so this button would not appear in these cases.

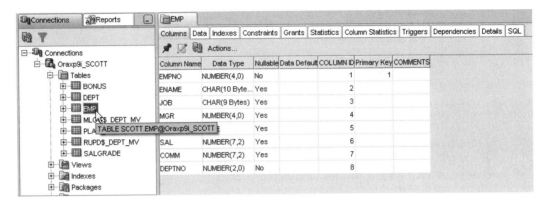

Columns Tab   The preceding image shows the EMP table column information. The edit button on the toolbar allows for columns to added, moved, and deleted (along with other table maintenance options; see the later heading "Edit Option").

Data Tab   The Data tab on the table information display allows for the data in the table object to be displayed, rows added, data changed, and rows deleted.
   The Data tab toolbar includes

- The freeze pin

- The refresh button

- "+" to open a row and allow rows to be added to the table

- An "X" to delete the row that the cursor is currently on

- Commit to write these changes to the database

- Rollback to not save any changes to the database

- The sort button to open a dialog box allowing for the data to be sorted by one or more columns

- The filter button to allow for where-clause syntax to be used to limit the rows returned

- An Actions button to allow for a variety of actions to be performed on the table (see the Actions context menu shown later under "Additional Display Tabs").

	EMP								

Columns | Data | Indexes | Constraints | Grants | Statistics | Column Statistics | Triggers | Dependencies | Details | SQL

Sort... Filter: Actions...

	EMPNO	ENAME	JOB	MGR	HIREDATE	SAL	COMM	DEPTNO
1	7839	KING	PRESIDENT		17-NOV-00	5000		10
2	7698	BLAKE	MANAGER	7839	01-MAY-81	2850		30
3	7782	CLARK	MANAGER	7839	09-JUN-81	2450		10
4	7566	JONES	MANAGER	7839	02-APR-81	2975		20
5	7654	MARTIN	SALESMAN	7698	28-SEP-81	1250	1400	30
6	7499	ALLEN	SALESMAN	7698	20-FEB-81	1600	300	30
7	7844	TURNER	SALESMAN	7698	08-SEP-81	1500	0	30
8	7900	JAMES	CLERK	7698	03-DEC-81	950		30

Notice next that the syntax "DEPTNO = 10" has been entered in the filter box and that now only rows with this data will appear. Also, when exporting this data now, only the rows displayed will be exported. Export is covered later in this chapter.

	EMP							

Columns | Data | Indexes | Constraints | Grants | Statistics | Column Statistics | Triggers | Dependencies | Details

Sort... Filter: DEPTNO = 10

	EMPNO	ENAME	JOB	MGR	HIREDATE	SAL	COMM	DEPTNO
1	7839	KING	PRESIDENT		17-NOV-00	5000		10
2	7782	CLARK	MANAGER	7839	09-JUN-81	2450		10
3	7934	MILLER	CLERK	7782	23-JAN-82	1300		10

Additional Display Tabs These are the remaining tabs on this display:

- The Indexes tab shows the indexes available, the columns they are created on, type of the index, the status, etc.

- The Constraints tab shows all the constraints on this table, the type of constraint, the referencing table, the status, and other statistical information.

- The Grants tab shows the privileges granted on this object to other users.

- The Statistics tab shows some useful statistics (including row count, block count, last analyzed time stamp, etc.), if statistics have been collected.

- The Column Statistics tab shows any histograms (and some useful histogram information such as low value, high value, and number of buckets), as well as a number of distinct values and other column-level statistics.

- The Triggers tab shows any triggers, the type of trigger, and the trigger status.

- The Dependencies tab shows all objects in the Oracle database that have a reference to this table. There is additional information at the bottom of this tab window that shows what objects in the database this object is related to.

■ The Details tab shows a variety of useful information about the object, including statistics, tablespace, storage parameters, etc.

■ The SQL tab shows the DDL for this object.

```
EMP
Columns | Data | Indexes | Constraints | Grants | Statistics | Column Statistics | Triggers | Dependencies | Details | SQL
     Actions...

REM SCOTT EMP

   CREATE TABLE "SCOTT"."EMP"
   (    "EMPNO" NUMBER(4,0) NOT NULL ENABLE,
        "ENAME" CHAR(10 BYTE),
        "JOB" CHAR(9 BYTE),
        "MGR" NUMBER(4,0),
        "HIREDATE" DATE,
        "SAL" NUMBER(7,2),
        "COMM" NUMBER(7,2),
        "DEPTNO" NUMBER(2,0) NOT NULL ENABLE,
         CONSTRAINT "EMP_PRIMARY_KEY" PRIMARY KEY ("EMPNO") ENABLE,
         CONSTRAINT "EMP_SELF_KEY" FOREIGN KEY ("MGR")
          REFERENCES "SCOTT"."EMP" ("EMPNO") ENABLE,
         CONSTRAINT "EMP_FOREIGN_KEY" FOREIGN KEY ("DEPTNO")
          REFERENCES "SCOTT"."DEPT" ("DEPTNO") ENABLE
   ) ;
```

Each database object has its own context menu of action items. These options are accessible in the Connections Navigator window or from the Actions button on the Object display window. All of these actions can be accessed via a right-mouse click on the Object Information display window as well. The next image shows all the available actions associated with a table object from the Connections Navigator.

Edit Option   The Table Edit option brings up the Edit Table dialog box, shown on the next page. Notice how similar this dialog box is to the Advanced Table Options dialog box shown under "Create Table Object" earlier. There is a tab that allows for additions and changes to any option of this table.

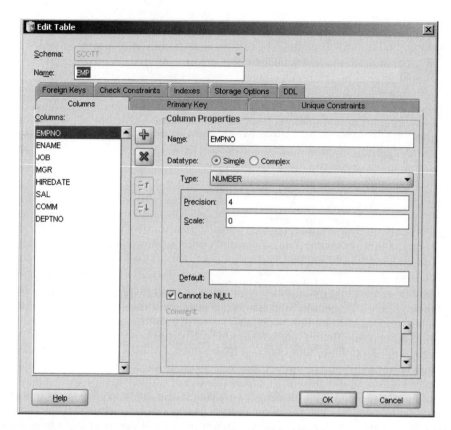

Table Option   The Table option on the context menu allows for a variety of functions to occur. Each function has its own dialog box. Most options will have a simple box prompting for the change with a tab to show the SQL.

TIP
The SQL in the SQL tab makes for a nice learning process about the syntax required for such changes. This syntax can always be copied and applied at a later time or given to the administrator with the proper permissions to execute the statement. Each of these dialog boxes has this SQL tab.

The image on the left next shows the various options associated with the table itself. Notice that the table can be renamed, copied, dropped, truncated, or locked, and comments can be added, parallel features added or changed, logging (journaling) mode changed, parallel features turned off, and a row count returned. These options each lead to a dialog box similar to the one shown on the right unless otherwise illustrated. Notice the SQL tab that shows the SQL required for the change.

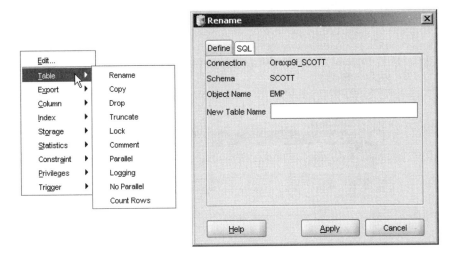

Export Option   The Table Export feature allows for the data in the table object to be saved in a variety of formats. This export option can also be accessed by a right-mouse click on the Table Information display window. Each of the selections will be applied to the radio group of similar selections in the Export Data dialog box. The type of export can be changed; the options in the drop-down menu correspond to those in the dialog box.

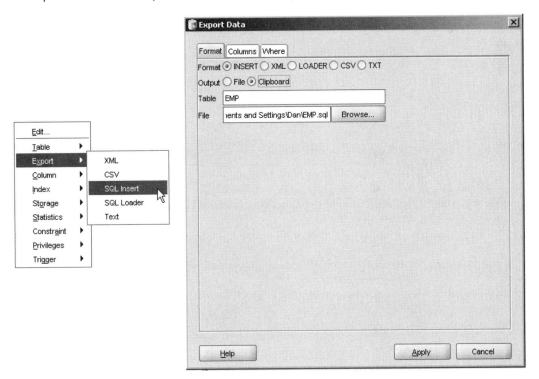

Notice the three tabs of the Export Data dialog box. This first tab of options allows for the type (format) of export to be performed and where to put the results (a file or the clipboard). Supported types are insert statements (as seen under the heading "Table Option"), XML, SQL*Loader, comma-separated values (CSV), and text. Notice that the clipboard option is selected for this example.

The Columns tab allows for the selection or exclusion of columns from the output. All is selected for this example so that the user doesn't have to manually select all of the columns.

All the data or a subset of the data can be exported from this operation. Apply a where clause using the Where Clause box to limit the data being returned in the Export Data dialog box Where tab. This example exports all of the rows.

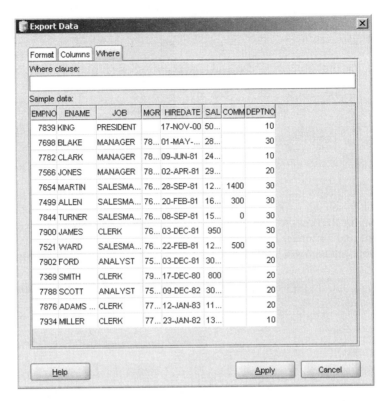

The next image shows the insert statements created by the Export Data dialog box operation and pasted into a Notepad window. These insert statements can easily be used to repopulate the table, or to prepare a script for a test environment.

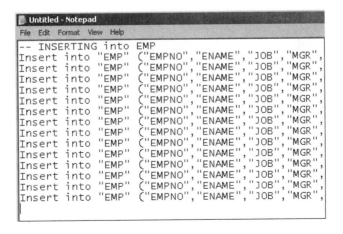

Column Option The Table Column selection allows for columns to be added, columns to be dropped, and columns to be normalized.

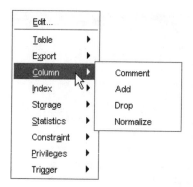

Each of these menu options gives access to a dialog box that has entry boxes for the required information for the request. The next image shows the dialog box for the Normalization option. Notice here that a primary key can be named, columns identified for normalization (columns separated out to their own tables), a sequence to be generated, and a trigger to be added.

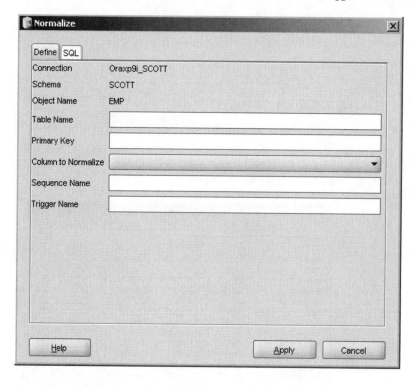

TIP

This is a powerful feature that allows for repeating values to be easily pulled out and added to their own table, establishing the correct referential integrity, and even moving the data! Normalizing data can greatly assist end users just looking for this kind of data and can save on data storage.

The SQL tab on this dialog box shows the extensive code required for this kind of change. SQL Developer is more than just a simple click-and-shoot tool; Oracle Corporation has given SQL Developer the appropriate "smarts" when necessary.

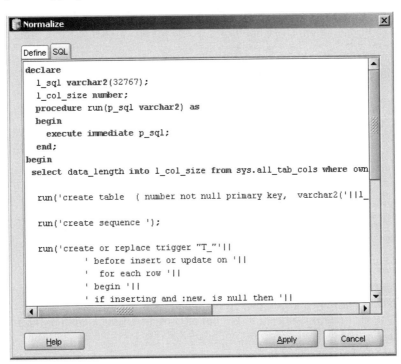

Index Option The Table Index Action context menu allows indexes to be created, dropped, or reorganized.

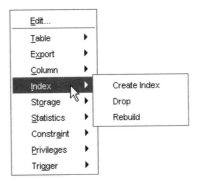

Storage Option The Table Storage context menu options provide access to a variety of storage operations available for the table. The operations include

- Shrinking the table (release unused extents)
- Enabling or disabling row movement (controls row migration)

- Enabling or disabling data compression within the table's data blocks
- Moving the table
- Moving the table to another tablespace
- Setting buffer cache options

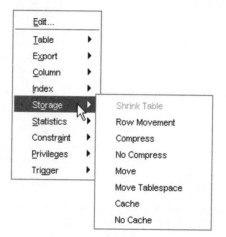

Statistics Option   The Statistics context menu has two options. Validate Structure verifies that all the blocks are valid and the rows within the blocks are formatted properly (i.e., they contain no corruption), and the Gather Statistics option uses the DBMS_STATS package to create statistics for this table. The dialog box for this option also allows for estimated statistics.

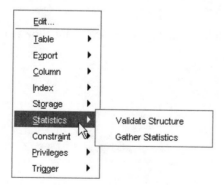

Constraint Option   The Constraint context menu options include

- The Enable Single and Disable Single options
- Provision for distinct constraints to be enabled or disabled
- Provision to drop constraints
- Provision to add constraint type check, primary key, foreign key, and unique constraints

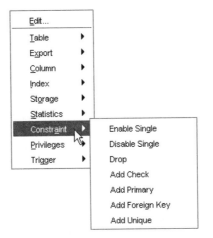

Privileges Option   The Privileges context menu option allows for privileges to be added (granted) or removed (revoked) using the interface shown to the right next. The Revoke dialog box is similar to the Grant dialog box but allows for some or all privileges to be deselected. The All check box applies all privileges to the users, and individuals or groups of users or roles can be selected for the privileges. Clicking Apply executes the grant or revocation of privileges selected.

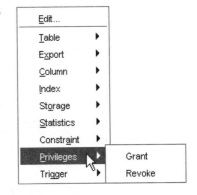

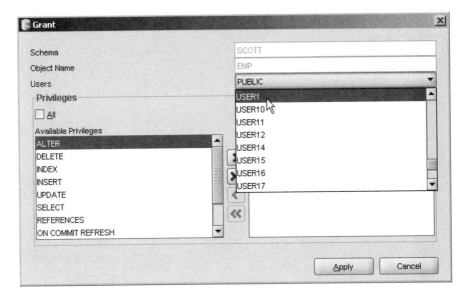

Trigger Option   The Trigger context menu option is the last of the Table context menu options. These options allow for

- Triggers to be created
- Primary key triggers to be created
- All triggers to be enabled or disabled
- Individual triggers to be enabled or disabled
- Triggers to be dropped

Create View Object

Views are virtual tables that can select data from one or more tables. Views are useful to hide columns from end users and to hide function, calculations, and other SQL complexities (such as complex join conditions between multiple tables) from the end users. In the Create View dialog box, SQL for a view can

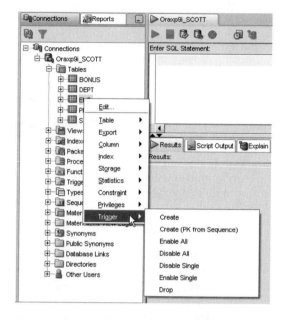

be copied and pasted into this dialog box. The View Information includes options to restrict the query and to 'force on create'. There is also the SQL tab to see the syntax created by this dialog box.

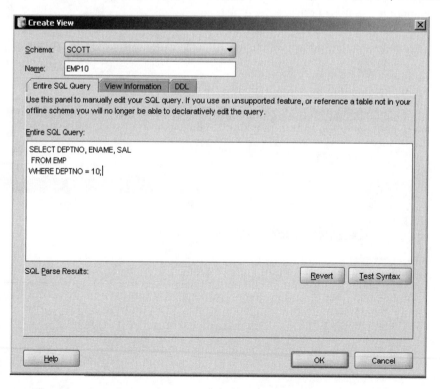

NOTE
Consult the Database SQL Reference Guide for specific details on any of these syntax options.

Working with View Objects

The Views Information display window has six tabs and the toolbar with the freeze data, edit, refresh, and Actions buttons. The available actions are discussed next in this chapter.

These are the features of the Views Information display window:

- The Columns tab shows the view's column information.

- The Data tab shows the data returned by the view.

- The Grants tab shows the privileges that have been granted to this view.

- The Dependencies tab has two areas showing any relationships this view has to other objects in the database and then any other objects that have relationships to this view.

- The Details tab shows a variety of information about the view, including the SQL that drives the view.

- The SQL tab shows the DDL for this view.

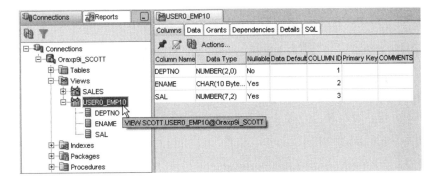

The next image shows all the available functionality associated with a view object:

- The Edit context menu option starts a dialog box similar to that for the Statistics options covered earlier.

- Rename allows the view to be renamed.

- Drop allows for the view to be deleted.

- Compile allows for the view to be compiled.

- Export has options similar to those for the Export options covered earlier.

- Privileges has options similar to those for the Privileges options covered earlier.

Create Index Object

Indexes allow for quick access to data in the table they are created for. The Create Index dialog box has three drop-down boxes. The Schema Owner allows SQL Developer to create indexes for other user accounts, with the correct permissions. Available tables in the selected schema are shown, as are the available columns in the table for indexing. Use the "+" and "−" buttons to add or change selections. Use the radio groups to select the type of index desired.

NOTE
Consult the Database SQL Reference Guide for specific details on any of these syntax options.

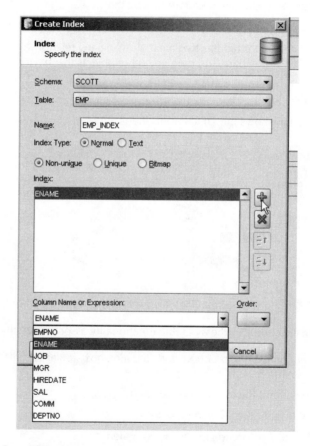

Working with Index Objects

The Index Information display window has four tabs of information and just the freeze data, refresh, and Actions buttons on its toolbar. The actions available are discussed next in this chapter.

These are the tabs:

- The Columns tab shows the column or columns involved with this index and the type of index (ascending or descending).

- The Details tab gives a variety of storage and statistical information about this index.

- The Statistics tab gives some useful statistics (if statistics have been collected) such as column granularity, number of levels, and number of leaf blocks, along with the last time statistics have been collected.

- The SQL tab shows the Oracle syntax of the index.

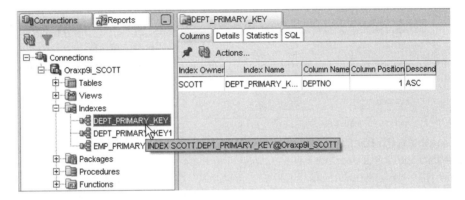

The next image shows all the available actions associated with an index object. The options include

- Drop
- Rebuild
- Rename
- Make unusable
- Coalesce
- Compute statistics

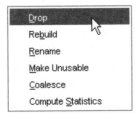

Create Package Object

Packages are a useful programming technique for sharing code, grouping similar procedures and functions together, etc. The Create Package dialog box prompts the user for a package name, and when OK is clicked, a PL/SQL code editor window is opened and the basic syntax for a package is inserted along with the package name just entered.

NOTE
Consult the Database PL/SQL Reference Guide for specific details on any of these syntax options.

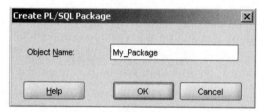 

Working with Package Objects

The Package object does not have a display information window, but each of the packages under this item does. The first image that follows shows the Package Spec Information display window, and the second image shows the Package Body Information display window. The toolbars are the same, including the freeze data, edit (which opens the code into the PL/SQL code editor interface), refresh, and Actions buttons. The actions include dropping the package, dropping the package body, and granting and revoking privileges. These options are discussed next in this chapter, along with the other Action context menu options. Both displays show the code on the Code tab, the permissions granted to this object on the Grants tab, both the dependencies this package has to other objects and those other objects have to this package on the Dependencies tab, and some useful information about the object on the Details tab.

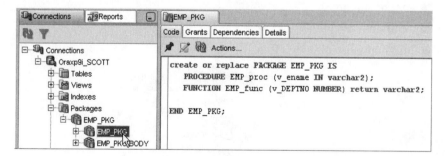

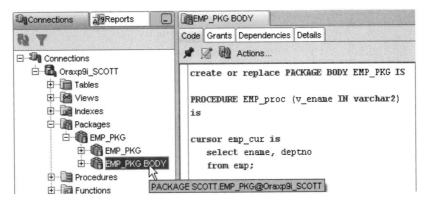

Click the Actions button or right-click the package object, the package name, or the package body to view several or all of these action options illustrated on the Package Action context menu. These are the package actions:

- The Open option opens the package or package body in a PL/SQL code editor window.

- The Compile and Compile For Debug options compile the package.

- The Run and Debug options open a dialog box prompting for any required parameters before executing the procedure or function within the package.

- The Execute Profile option creates a PL/SQL profile.

- The Drop Package, Drop Package Body, Grant, and Revoke options all open dialog boxes to perform the respective tasks. The Grant and Revoke dialog boxes will be similar to the one shown earlier under "Privileges Option."

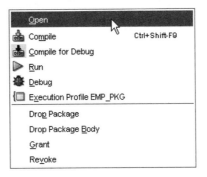

Create Procedure Object

Procedures are stored PL/SQL routines. The first image that follows shows the Create Procedure dialog box. This dialog box prompts the user for the procedure name and any parameters required by the procedure. Clicking OK opens a PL/SQL code editor window with the basic PL/SQL procedure syntax.

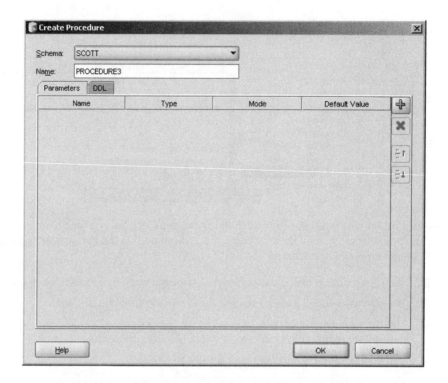

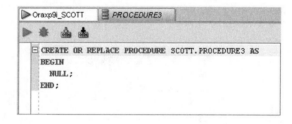

NOTE
Consult the Database PL/SQL Reference Guide for specific details on any of these syntax options.

Working with Procedure Objects

The Procedure Information display window has the same features and options as illustrated earlier under "Working with Package Objects."

The Procedure Objects context menu is illustrated next. These are the options:

■   The Open option opens a PL/SQL code editor window and puts the procedure's PL/SQL code into the editor.

■   The Compile and Compile For Debug options simply execute with no additional dialog boxes.

■   The Run and Debug options open a parameter dialog box and then execute.

■   The Execution Profile option runs a PL/SQL profile.

■   The options to Grant and Revoke privileges open a dialog box similar to the one already illustrated under "Privileges Option."

■   The Drop option deletes the procedure.

■   The Compile Dependents option compiles all related objects.

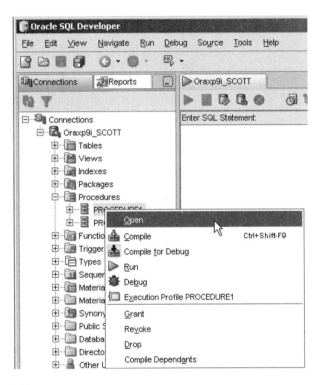

Create Function Object

Functions are stored PL/SQL routines that can be used in SQL statements. The Create Function dialog box prompts the user for the function name and any parameters required by the function. Clicking OK opens a PL/SQL code editor window with the basic PL/SQL function syntax.

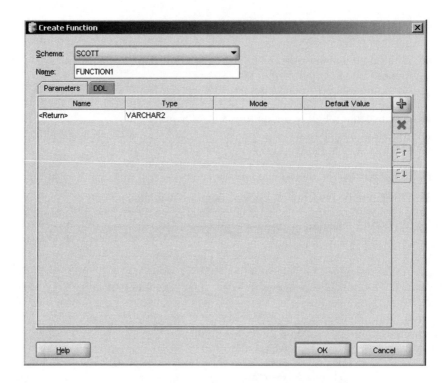

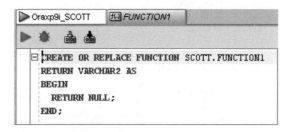

NOTE
Consult the Database PL/SQL Reference Guide for specific details on any of these syntax options.

Working with Function Objects

The Functions Information display window has the same features and options as already illustrated under "Working with Package Objects."

The Function Actions Objects context menu includes these options:

- The Open option opens a PL/SQL code editor window and puts the function's PL/SQL code into the editor.

- The Run and Debug options open a parameter dialog box and then execute.

- The Execution Profile option runs a PL/SQL profile.

- The Grant and Revoke privileges options open a dialog box similar to one shown earlier under "Privileges Option."

- Drop is used to delete the function.

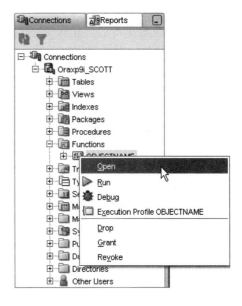

Create Trigger Object

Triggers are PL/SQL modules that execute according to the DML activity of the table or object they are assigned to. The Create Trigger dialog box includes options to name the trigger, to assign it to a type of database object, to assign it to a named database object (such as a table), and to specify the type of execution desired (before or after the DML operation, the type of DML operation, and whether for one execution per DML operation or for each row affected by the DML operation). There is a dialog box for the old and new values of the object affected, columns affected, and conditions of execution. There is also the DDL tab to see the syntax created by this dialog box.

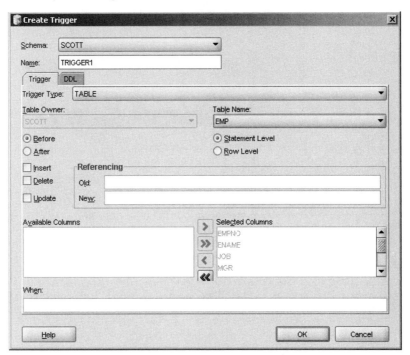

NOTE
Consult the Database SQL Reference Guide for specific details on any of these syntax options.

Working with Trigger Objects

The Triggers Information display window has the same features and options as already shown under "Working with Package Objects."

The Trigger Object context menu includes these options:

- The Open option opens a PL/SQL code editor window and puts the trigger's PL/SQL code into the editor.

- The Compile and Compile For Debug options simply execute with no additional dialog boxes.

- The Execution Profile option runs a PL/SQL profile.

- The Edit option works just like the Open option, opening a PL/SQL code editor window and putting the trigger's code into the window.

- The Rename option renames the trigger.

- The Drop option deletes the trigger.

- The Enable and Disable options enable or disable the trigger.

Create Types Object

The Oracle RDBMS allows for custom data types or user-defined data types. In the Create Type dialog box, when you click OK, a PL/SQL code editor window opens and basic PL/SQL code is created for the Type definition.

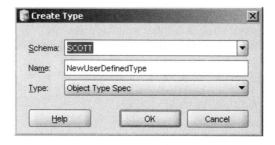

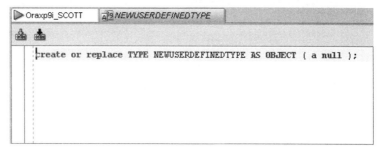

NOTE
Consult the Database SQL Reference Guide for specific details on any
of these syntax options.

Working with Type Objects

The Type Information display window has the same features and options as you have already
encountered under "Working with Package Objects."

There is only one option on the Type Actions context menu, and that is to edit the package
spec/body. When this option is selected, the code associated with the type is opened in a PL/SQL
code editor window.

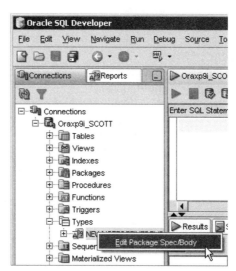

Create Sequence Object

Sequences are features that return a number when accessed via SQL. The Create Database Sequence dialog box has entry boxes for all the required information, as well as a DDL tab to see the syntax created by this dialog box.

NOTE
Consult the Database SQL Reference Guide for specific details on any of these syntax options.

Working with Sequence Objects

The Sequence Information display window has three tabs and has the same four buttons on the toolbar (freeze view, edit, refresh, and Actions).

The first tab shows the initialization details of the sequence, the second tab shows the other objects that this sequence is dependent upon and objects that depend on this sequence, and the SQL tab shows the DDL useful to recreate this sequence.

There is only a Drop option on the Actions button, which opens a dialog box prompting to drop the selected sequence.

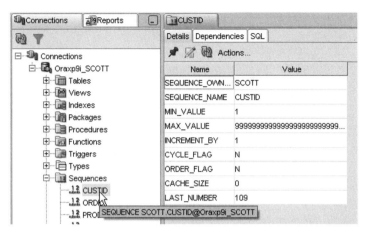

There are only two options on the Sequence Actions context menu. The Edit option opens a dialog box similar to the one just shown under "Create Sequence Object," allowing changes to any of the fields, and the Drop option drops the sequence.

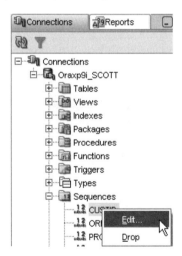

Create Materialized View Object

Materialized views are database objects that contain the results of a query. They are used to store data in summary form (for performance enhancements) and can be used to create subsets of data. The Create Materialized View Connections Navigator context option starts the three-tab dialog box by the same name. This dialog box allows for the entry of the SQL statement that the materialized view will be focused on. The Materialized View Information tab includes all the materialized view options. Open the DDL tab to see the syntax created by the other tabs.

NOTE
Consult the Database SQL Reference Guide for specific details on any of these syntax options.

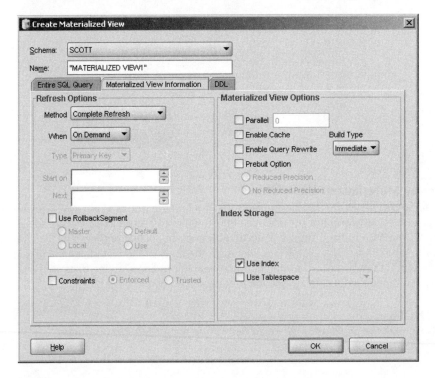

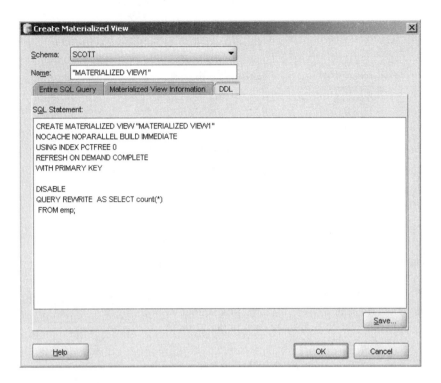

Working with Materialized View Objects

The Materialized View Information display window has seven tabs and four buttons on its toolbar. These buttons are freeze view, edit (which starts a dialog box similar to that in the preceding section), refresh, and Actions. The Actions options are discussed next.

The display tabs are as follows:

- The Columns tab shows the column and column information.

- The Data tab shows the data returned by the materialized view. This tab has the sort and filter operations but does not allow the data to be manipulated.

- The Indexes tab shows any indexes on the materialized view or the table that the materialized view is associated with.

- The Grants tab shows the privileges associated with this materialized view.

- The Details tab contains a great deal of storage and statistical information about this materialized view.

- The SQL tab shows the syntax useful to recreate this materialized view.

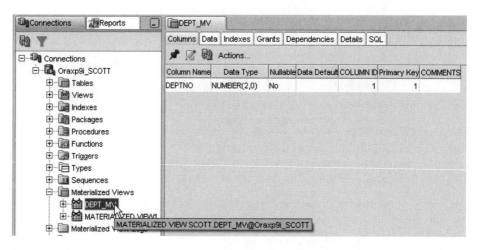

The Materialized View Actions context menu has these options:

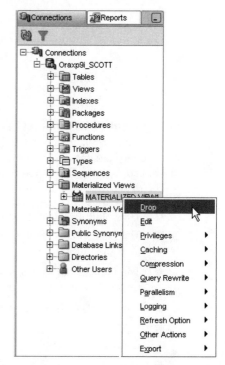

- The Drop option deletes the materialized view.

- The Edit option opens a dialog box similar to the one you have already seen under "Create Materialized View Object."

- The Privileges option has two suboptions (Grant and Revoke), both of which open a dialog box similar to the one under the earlier heading "Index Option."

- The Caching, Compression, Query Rewrite, Parallelism, and Logging options all have a submenu for enabling or disabling the option.

- The Refresh option has a submenu that allows the refresh method and the refresh type to be altered.

- The Other Actions option allows you to shrink the materialized view, create a materialized view log, and compile/refresh/rebuild materialized views.

- The Export option starts a dialog similar to the one shown previously in this chapter under "Export Option."

Working with Materialized View Logs

Materialized View logs are created via the Materialized View actions context menu option Other Actions | Create Materialized View Log.

The Materialized View Log Information display window has five tabs and four buttons on its toolbar. The Columns tab shows the columns associated with the materialized view log. The Grants tab shows the privileges associated with this object. The Dependencies tab shows what objects this object is dependent upon and also what objects are dependent upon this object. The Details tab shows useful information, including the materialized view log table name. The SQL tab shows the SQL syntax for this object.

The buttons on the toolbar are freeze view, edit, refresh, and Actions. The actions options are discussed next in this section.

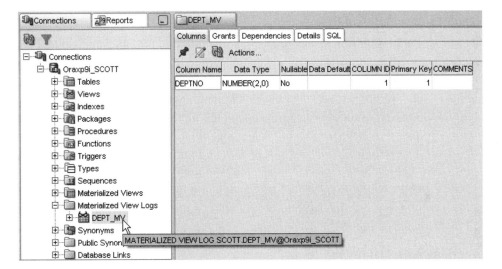

The Materialized View context menu options simply drop the materialized view log or add parallel options to the materialized view the log is associated with.

NOTE
Consult the Database SQL Reference Guide for specific details on any of these syntax options.

Create Synonym Object

Synonyms are a way of creating alternative names for a variety of database objects. In the Create Database Synonym dialog box (see the next page), notice the Public check box. If this is checked, then the synonym appears and will be maintained by the Public Synonym Connections Navigator object (next in the list). The DDL tab shows the syntax created by this dialog box.

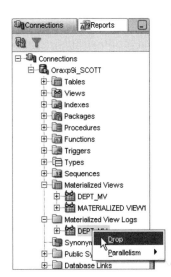

NOTE
Consult the Database SQL Reference Guide for specific details on any of these syntax options.

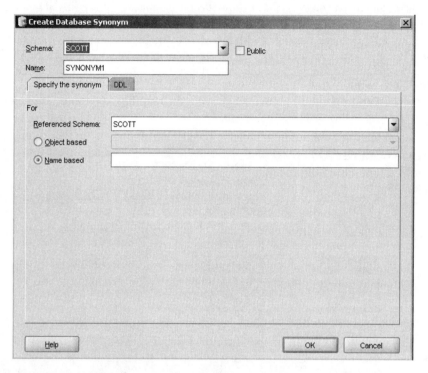

Working with Synonyms

The Synonyms Information display window is illustrated next. Notice it only has the two tabs: one displaying information about the synonym and the SQL tab showing the syntax for the synonym. There are three buttons on this window's toolbar: freeze view, refresh, and Actions. The Actions options are discussed next.

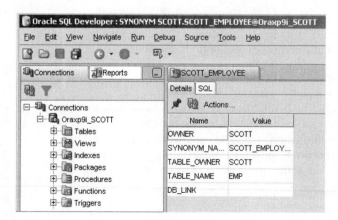

Notice there are only two Synonyms Actions context menu options: Rename the synonym and Drop the synonym. Both options starts a dialog box that also has the SQL tab showing the syntax used to implement the desired request.

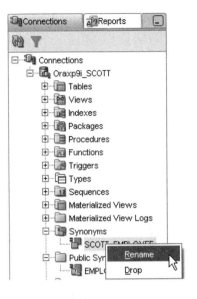

Working with Public Synonyms

Checking the Public check box in the Create Database Synonym dialog box shown previously creates public synonyms. Public synonyms are visible to all users of the instance. The information display and the Public Synonyms Actions context menu options are the same as shown in the preceding section.

Create Database Link Object

Database *links* allow easy access to data on other Oracle database instances. The Create Database Link dialog box allows public links to be created and allows other users to use the links as well. There is also the DDL tab to see the syntax created by this dialog box.

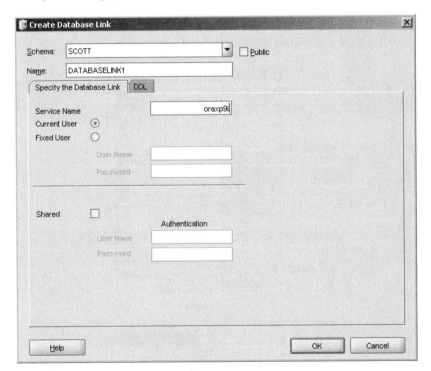

NOTE
Consult the Database SQL Reference Guide for specific details on any of these syntax options.

Working with Database Links

The Database Link Information display window has the same tabs and toolbar buttons as you saw under "Working with Synonyms." Two action options are available for database links: Test Database Link or Drop the link. Both options start a dialog box that has a SQL tab showing the SQL used to implement the request.

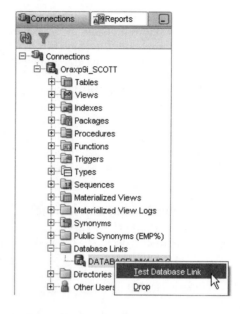

Directories Object

This Connections Navigator option simply displays any existing database directories. There are currently no options to create or filter these from SQL Developer.

Other Users Object

The final object is the Other Users object. This option allows all other users on the Oracle instance to be viewed in the same Connections Navigator tree options just discussed. This functionality is equivalent to "SELECT * FROM ALL_USERS" in SQL*Plus. The other user accounts are displayed, but the proper privileges are still required to view any of the other users' objects.

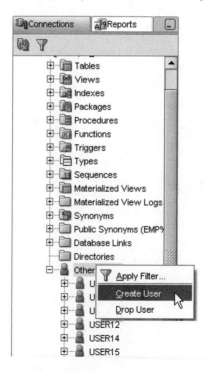

The Connections Navigator context menu allows user objects to be filtered, created, or dropped. The Create User option opens a dialog box that allows additional users to be added to the instance.

NOTE
Consult the Database SQL Reference Guide for specific details on any of these syntax options.

Working with Other Users

The Other Users Information display window has two tabs that show some basic user information and the SQL syntax for creating the user, along with three buttons that freeze the view, edit the user (starts the Create Users dialog box just shown), and refresh the screen. This final option is shown here.

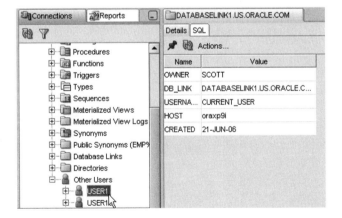

Summary

The Connections Navigator is the interface that gives easy access to each of the supported database object types and to the interfaces designed to best exploit creating and maintaining those database objects. Each database object has its own unique features and requirements, and SQL Developer addresses each feature with custom dialog boxes that always show the SQL used to implement the desired feature or change.

CHAPTER
6

Working with SQL

he SQL language is the heart of any relational database. SQL Developer makes working with SQL, SQL*Plus scripts, and PL/SQL a snap. This chapter will cover the SQL worksheet interface. This interface has many code-enhancing features.

SQL Developer allows for the easy access, development, and execution of SQL stored in files, in the middle of scripts, etc. SQL Developer has insights that allow for quick access to objects, parameters, and columns with simple keyboard signals. SQL Developer also has code templates as well as a SQL history. This chapter will cover all of the features of the SQL worksheet interface.

The SQL Worksheet Interface

The SQL worksheet interface (see Figure 6-1) is a nice GUI interface for working with SQL, PL/SQL blocks, and SQL scripts. SQL Developer opens a SQL worksheet interface automatically when a connection is established to a database. Additional SQL worksheet windows can be opened by using the SQL Worksheet button on the SQL Developer toolbar, or by right-clicking a database connection in the Connections Navigator window and selecting Open SQL Worksheet.

Figure 6-1 illustrates the SQL Developer environment with the SQL worksheet interface open. Notice the SQL area is the upper area in the SQL worksheet and the lower area is for the output from various types of code executions. Also notice the location of the various toolbars useful in working with SQL.

There are several ways to do just about anything in SQL Developer: by using a menu item from the SQL Developer Menu toolbar, by making a selection from a pop-up menu (accessed via a right-click), using a button on one of the toolbars, or by pressing a function key (or predetermined keystroke combination). The results of the query will appear in the Results tab, and the execution time will appear next to the SQL worksheet toolbar. SQL execution is also available via a pop-up menu from a right-click. If there is more than one SQL statement in the window, make sure the cursor is on the SQL statement to be executed and press F9 or the Execute Statement button on the SQL worksheet toolbar. If all SQL or a SQL script is to be executed, click the Run Script button on the SQL worksheet toolbar, or press F5. Highlight a single SQL statement and use the F5 key or Run Script when multiple SQL statements are in the window and only one is desired to be run as a script. The output from this operation will appear in the Script Output tab of the SQL worksheet interface.

The buttons on the SQL worksheet toolbar (from left to right) are

- **Execute Statement (F9)**   Places the cursor on the SQL to be executed. The result set is displayed in the Results output tab.

- **Run Script (F5)**   Runs all SQL (or just the highlighted SQL) and some SQL*Plus commands in the window. The output is displayed in the Scripts Output output tab.

- **Commit (F2)**   Saves data changes from the executed SQL to the database.

- **Rollback (F3)**   Undoes data changes from the executed SQL.

- **Cancel (CTRL-Q)**   SQL Developer allows for the canceling of long-running SQL!

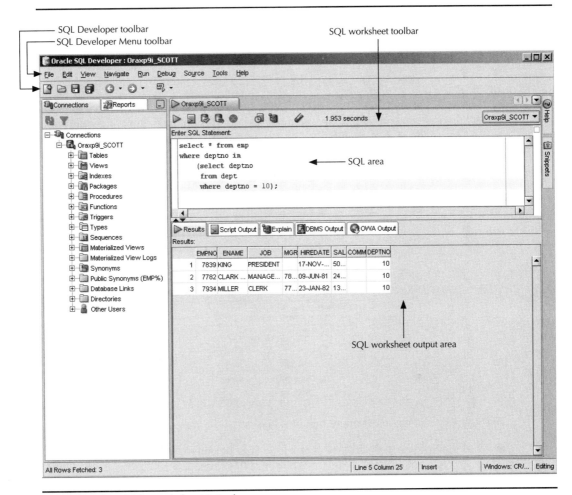

SQL Developer toolbar
SQL Developer Menu toolbar
SQL worksheet toolbar

SQL area

SQL worksheet output area

FIGURE 6-1. *SQL worksheet interface*

- **SQL History (F8)** Invokes the SQL History interface. This interface is discussed later in this chapter.

- **Execute Explain Plan (F6)** Populates the Explain tab in the output area.

- **Clear (CTRL-D)** Clears the SQL worksheet.

The SQL Developer toolbar buttons (from left to right) are

- New (for connections)

- Open (code from a file on the file system)

- Save (contents of current interface tab)

- Save All (saves contents of all interface tabs)

- Back and forward buttons to walk through the available tabs
- Open SQL worksheet (opens a new SQL worksheet tab and prompts for the connection to associate it with)

The SQL worksheet commands are also available via the context menu (a right-click in the SQL worksheet window). Notice in the menu that follows that the function keys and keystroke combinations are also available for each of these commands. Appendix A of this book cross-references all preassigned function keys and keystroke combinations.

The SQL worksheet context menu includes these items:

- Execute Statement (F9) will execute a lone SQL statement in the SQL area or a selected SQL statement in the SQL area. Results from this execution will be displayed in the Results tab in the output area.

- Execute Explain Plan (F6) will populate the Explain Plan tab in the output area with an execution plan from the SQL selected in the SQL area.

- Run Script (F5) selection will execute all SQL (or just highlighted SQL statements) and associated statements in the SQL area and display the output in the Scripts Output tab in the output area.

- Open File (CTRL-O) will open a file system box and allow for files containing SQL and SQL scripts to be opened.

- Save File (CTRL-S) will save the contents of the SQL area to the file where it was opened. If a file is not associated with the SQL area, then a dialog box will open and the filename and location information can be supplied. This is the same dialog box as if the menu item File | Save As was selected.

- Print (CTRL-P) will send the contents of the SQL worksheet to the default printer.

- Clear (CTRL-D) will clear all text from the SQL area.

- Cancel (CTRL-Q) is used to stop execution of a SQL statement.

- SQL History (F8) will open the SQL History interface. This interface is discussed later in this chapter.

- Cut (CTRL-X), copy (CTRL-C), paste (CTRL-V), and select all (CTRL-A) operations are also available from this pop-up menu.

- Format SQL (CTRL-B) will format the SQL in the SQL area.

- Export will start the Data Export dialog, again, discussed later in this chapter.

Entering, Accessing, and Executing SQL

SQL Developer will allow SQL to be pasted in from the clipboard, opened (using File | Open, or the toolbar open button, or CTRL-O), or double-clicked from the file system. When SQL Developer is executed for the first time, SQL Developer will prompt to associate all .SQL files with SQL Developer. If Yes is selected, then double-clicking SQL files using the Windows Explorer (on a PC for example) will start SQL Developer, open a SQL worksheet, and put the contents of the file into the SQL worksheet window.

SQL Developer allows you to execute more than one SQL statement at a time or to run SQL*Plus scripts. These scripts can include PL/SQL blocks and some SQL*Plus commands. As seen next, the SQL*Plus commands are noted but not executed.

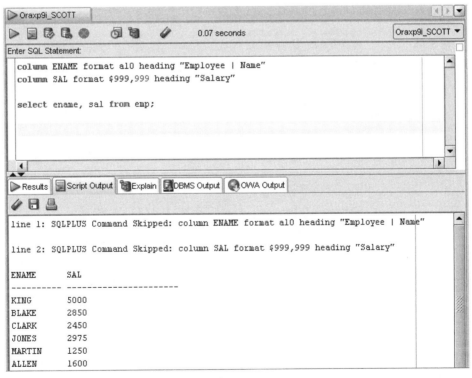

TIP
To see all the SQL*Plus output, use this three-step method: Make your changes using SQL Developer, save the script to a file, and in SQL*Plus simply type **start <filename>.sql** *to see all the SQL*Plus commands and intended output.*

To execute the contents of the SQL worksheet as a script, press F5 or click the Execute Script button on the SQL worksheet toolbar. Use this button to execute more than one SQL statement or function at the same time. The output is displayed in the SQL Script output tab.

TIP
The SQL worksheet can also execute the Start, "@," and describe commands. For example: START C:\TEMP\MyScript.SQL will execute this script and put the output in the Script Output tab.

Executing PL/SQL

PL/SQL code can be executed through the SQL worksheet with the Execute (F9) or Run Script (F5) commands. Any DBMS_OUTPUT will be displayed in the DBMS_OUTPUT tab. PL/SQL functions are included in the text of the SQL statement or by variable assignment in PL/SQL. The next image shows the execution and output of a simple PL/SQL block. Make sure to "enable DBMS Output" by clicking the left-most button on the DBMS Output tab toolbar prior to executing the PL/SQL routine with DBMS_OUTPUT.

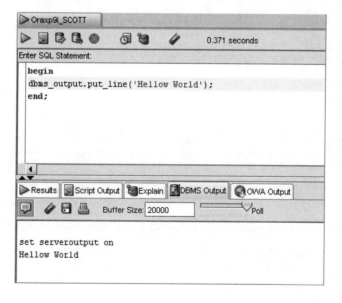

NOTE
All commands executed have feedback that can be seen in the lower-left corner of SQL Developer. The most common feedback is "Statement Processed."

Creating SQL without Typing

SQL Developer can easily create a working SQL statement that includes all of the columns of a particular table. Later in this chapter, you will see how to create INSERT statements from data in the Results tab. This section will also illustrate using code templates called snippets. SQL Developer will also help with lists of objects, lists of columns, lists of procedures/functions, and lists of options and parameters of parameters/functions. These lists are called code insights and code completion insights.

SQL from the Connections Navigator

SQL Developer can easily create a full SELECT statement, with all the columns, for any table. Simply drag a table name from the Connections Navigator tables item and drop it into the SQL worksheet. Figure 6-2 illustrates the SQL generated when the DEPT table is dragged from the Connections Navigator and dropped into the SQL area of the SQL worksheet.

SQL and PL/SQL from Code Snippets

Code snippets are code templates, code shortcuts, various functions, and optimizer hints that are available in an autohide window (Minimize). The snippet window can be undocked (Float) from the SQL Developer interface.

Code snippets are started from the View | Snippets menu item. Minimize the Snippets interface to have it autohide, move it to the left side or the right side of the SQL Developer interface with a drag-and-drop operation, or undock it using a right-click on the Snippets interface and selecting the Float option. Visit Chapter 4 for topics on docking, minimizing, and undocking the various SQL Developer assistants.

The image on the next page shows the LEADING optimizer hint being added to the SQL statement from Figure 6-2. All snippets have a description that will appear by hovering the mouse over the snippet item. Snippets are added to the SQL worksheet window via a drag-and-drop operation.

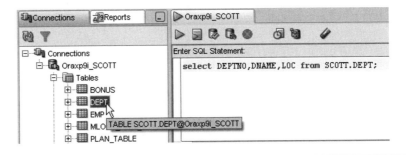

FIGURE 6-2. *Automatic SQL statement generation*

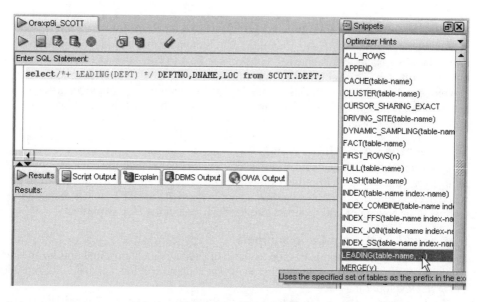

The code snippets are organized into ten categories. These categories are available by clicking the right side of the title bar of the Snippets panel and selecting the category from the drop-down menu.

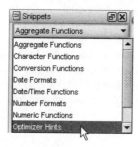

 NOTE
SQL Developer version 1.1 offers you the ability to add your own snippets and additional categories. Use the toolbar or the context menu associated with the Snippet window.

The next image shows the available aggregate functions.

The common character functions are illustrated next.

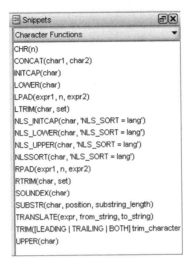

The next image shows the conversion functions.

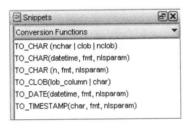

A few of the date formats are available using the Date Formats as shown next. There are enough combinations illustrated to show a number of the available date masks.

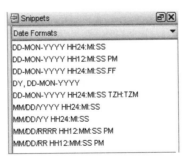

Various Date/Time Functions are illustrated next.

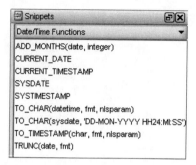

The next image shows the number formats available in the Snippets panel.

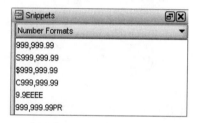

Several numeric functions are illustrated next.

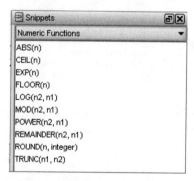

The Snippets panel has many optimizer hints. Most of these are illustrated next.

There are more than a dozen PL/SQL code templates in the Snippets panel. See the next image for the available templates in this version of SQL Developer.

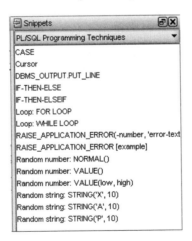

The next image shows a dozen various pseudocolumns.

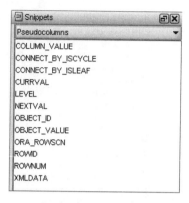

NOTE

Be sure to check future versions of SQL Developer for additional categories and additional snippets in each of the categories.

Code Insights

Code insights are pop-up boxes of table, packages, procedures, and/or function information. Code insights are triggered by a single "." after the table name or package name. The columns will appear in a pop-up box for a table code insight, and the available functions and procedures in a package will appear after a package name.

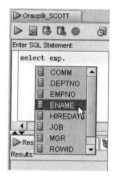

The keystroke combination CTRL-SPACE will also signal the code insights. The image to the right shows the code insights for the table EMP.

The next image illustrates the package code insights.

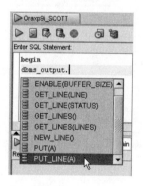

TIP

If you typed in DBMS_OUTPUT.P and then pressed CTRL-SPACE, the insight would show just the functions starting with a P!

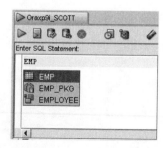

Code completion insights show all available objects (tables, views, packages, procedures, and/or functions) for a string. This image shows the results of entering the string "EMP" followed by pressing CTRL-SPACE. The various objects that start with EMP are shown.

Miscellaneous SQL Topics

This section will wrap up the remaining topics associated with the SQL area of the SQL worksheet window. SQL Developer saves all executed SQL statements (using Execute Statement or F9) in a history file called SQL History. SQL statements can also be nicely formatted, indenting the columns and where clauses and putting most everything on its own line for readability. The file save feature is also illustrated in this section.

SQL History

SQL History is a nice feature that saves the SQL executed (with either Execute Statement or F9) in the SQL worksheet for future reference. SQL History is accessed by using the F8 key or by clicking the SQL History button on the SQL worksheet toolbar. The next image shows the SQL History interface. Notice that additional information such as the entire SQL text can be viewed by hovering over the item of interest. Load the selected SQL into the SQL area by selecting one of two options at the bottom of the SQL History window: Replace (to clear the SQL worksheet and add the SQL) or Append (to add the SQL at the end of the existing code in the SQL worksheet). The Clear button empties the SQL History. There is a filter option to help find the SQL statement with specific strings (such as a table name, perhaps).

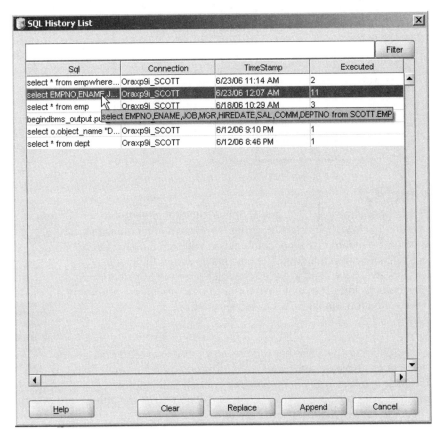

TIP
Using the Sort field on the SQL field will make specific SQL statements easier to find.

SQL Formatting

SQL Developer can format SQL in the SQL area for better readability, indenting the code and putting everything on its own line. The image on the left shows an unformatted SQL statement and the pop-up menu from a right-click from the SQL area, and the image on the right shows the same SQL statement after formatting.

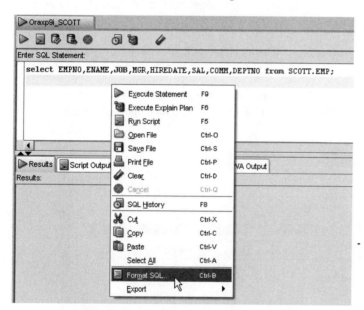

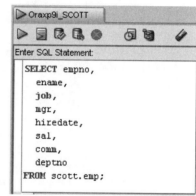

Saving SQL

SQL Developer allows for SQL and scripts in the SQL area to be saved either back to their originating files (save) or to other filenames (save as). The standard CTRL-S key combination will signal a save for the current SQL worksheet window. The next image shows the menu choices for Save, Save As, and Save All (which saves all SQL in any of SQL Developer's interfaces that have unsaved changes). There are Save and Save All buttons on the SQL Developer toolbar.

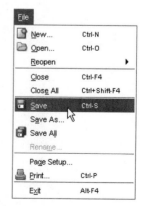

NOTE
If the SQL, script, or code has not previously been saved, a dialog box will be displayed asking for a file location and a filename. If the code had previously been saved or opened from another file, then the Save and Save All operations will simply write the new code into the originally defined files.

The Save and Save As dialog boxes (Save is shown next; the dialog boxes are the same, though) provide for not only a filename to be given but for a location to be specified as well. The Home button will put the path of SQL Developer into the Location box; the User button will put the user's home document location into the Location box. Use the buttons on the upper right to navigate the file system, create a new folder, and either list or show details of other files with a .SQL suffix in the specified location.

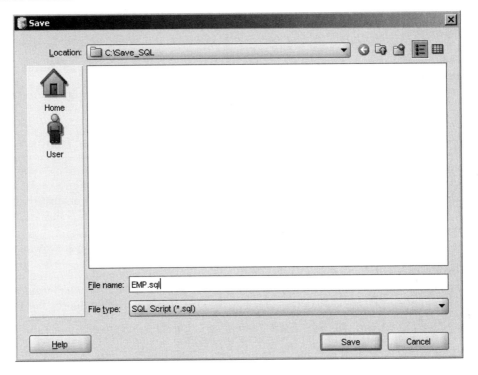

Notice that when the contents of the SQL worksheet are saved, the tab changes from the connection user ID to the name of the file. If a file is opened from the computer, its name appears in this tab as well and the toolbar buttons remain grayed out until a database connection is associated with the opened tab.

SQL Output

The output from code executed is displayed in the output area in one of five tabs, depending on the type of output generated by the code in the SQL area and the type of execution selected. The next image shows the SQL worksheet output area.

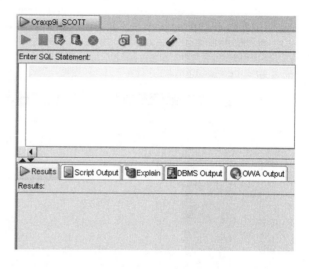

The Results tab is the output from a single SQL statement execution (by clicking the Execute Statement button or pressing F9). The Scripts Output is populated when you click the Run Script button or press F5 key. The Explain tab is populated when you click Execute Explain Plan or press F6. The DBMS Output and the OWA Output are populated depending on the type of SQL being executed in the SQL area. If there are DBMS_OUTPUT statements in the code, then the DBMS Output area will be populated (after you first go to the tab and click Set Serveroutput On), and the OWA Output tab will be populated if the code being executed contains any web-function output.

Several of the tabs have their own toolbars and special operations that are available.

The Results Tab

The Results tab is the output from a single SQL statement execution. The next image shows the results from the SQL generated from dragging the DEPT table name into the SQL area.

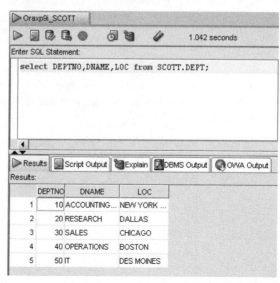

The Export option as seen next pertains to this output tab. The Export feature here works the same as the Data tab from the Table Information display illustrated in Chapter 5.

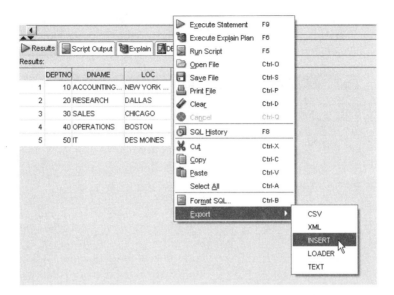

The next image shows the Export Data dialog box. The selection from the pop-up menu is selected in the Format radio group. This export is for Insert statements, so a table name is needed in the Table box; otherwise, the table name part of the syntax would be left out of the resulting generated code.

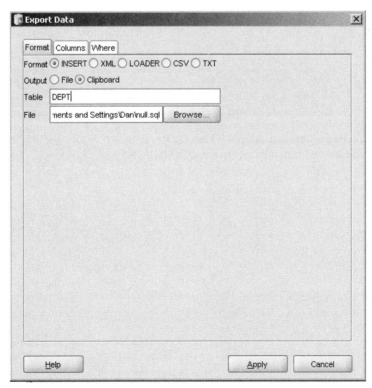

Other export options, such as Text, do not need the Table name. Select the desired output type (file or clipboard), the columns to be included (on the Columns tab), and any where clause to include only certain rows in the output.

The next image shows a sample where clause. As when working with the Data tab, include the where clause text but without the keyword "where."

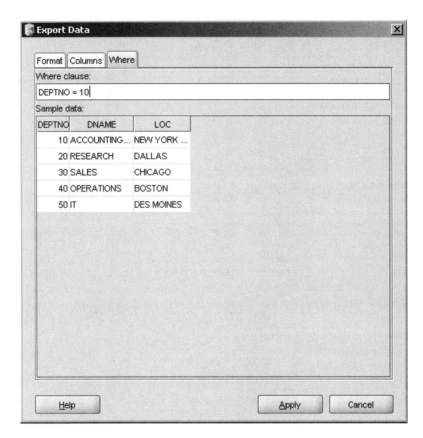

The next image shows the generated SQL statements using Notepad.

```
Untitled - Notepad
File  Edit  Format  View  Help
-- INSERTING into DEPT
Insert into "DEPT" ("DEPTNO","DNAME","LOC") values (10,'ACCOUNTING    ','NEW YORK    ');
Insert into "DEPT" ("DEPTNO","DNAME","LOC") values (20,'RESEARCH      ','DALLAS      ');
Insert into "DEPT" ("DEPTNO","DNAME","LOC") values (30,'SALES         ','CHICAGO     ');
Insert into "DEPT" ("DEPTNO","DNAME","LOC") values (40,'OPERATIONS    ','BOSTON      ');
Insert into "DEPT" ("DEPTNO","DNAME","LOC") values (50,'IT            ','DES MOINES  ');
```

The Script Output Tab

The Script Output tab (see the next page) shows the output from a Run Script or F5 type of
execution. Notice the three toolbar buttons that will clear the output, save the output to a file, or
send the output to the default printer.

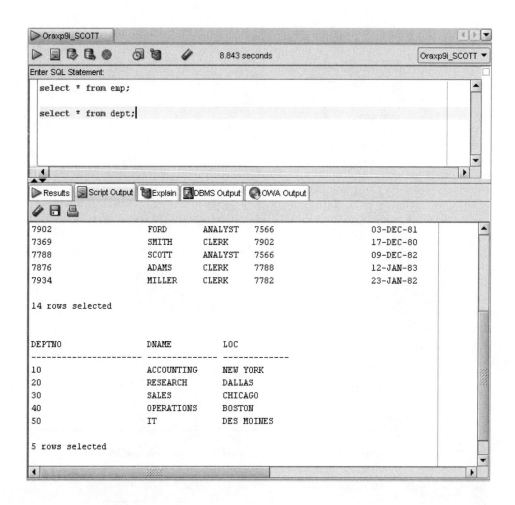

The Explain Plan Tab

SQL Developer can run an explain plan for the selected SQL statement in the SQL area. Simply click Explain Plan on the SQL worksheet toolbar or press F6 to see the explain plan. Notice that the columns appearing in this output area can be moved for better viewing of important columns.

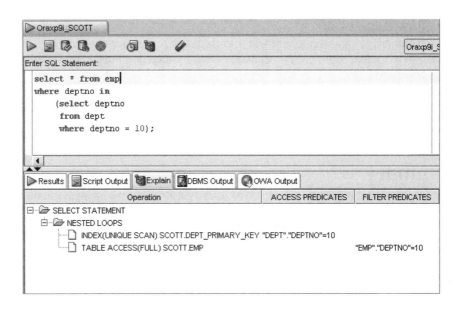

TIP
Starting with Oracle9 release 2, the where clause and filtering predicates are now populated in the Plan_Table. Notice in this display that I have shuffled the columns so that these useful columns appear in the display!

The DBMS Output Tab

The DBMS Output tab displays any DBMS output from any PL/SQL that was executed using Execute Statement or the F9 key. If you click Run Script or press F5, the output will be displayed in the Script Output tab. Notice that there are six options on the tab's toolbar. Left to right, they are

- Enable output (required to be on before DBMS_OUTPUT will be displayed)
- Clear tab display
- Save to a file
- Print to the default print
- Set the DBMS output buffer size
- Poll the DBMS output area. This poll value is the frequency with which SQL Developer will check to see if there is any new DBMS_OUTPUT to display.

The OWA Output Tab

This tab will display any web-type PL/SQL calls that SQL Developer encounters. There are four buttons on its toolbar: Enable OWA Output (must be turned on prior to encountering OWA code), Clear, Save, and Print.

Summary

The SQL worksheet interface is the main SQL Developer interface for working with SQL, SQL scripts (including a selection of SQL*Plus scripts), and scripts that contain PL/SQL blocks of code. This interface has many features that can easily enhance coding productivity (code snippets, code insights, drag-and-drop SQL, etc.). This chapter took an in-depth look at each of the available features of the SQL worksheet.

CHAPTER
7

Working with PL/SQL

QL Developer allows for the easy creation and maintenance of Oracle PL/SQL packages, procedures, functions, and database triggers. This chapter will work with PL/SQL and the PL/SQL editor interface. Chapter 5 illustrated how easy it is to create database PL/SQL-type objects, and Chapter 6 showed PL/SQL coding techniques in the form of code snippets. This chapter illustrates how to use these features to enhance PL/SQL coding and illustrates the SQL Developer PL/SQL debugger.

The SQL Developer PL/SQL Editor Interface

The PL/SQL tabbed detail display is automatically started when a PL/SQL package, procedure, function, or database trigger is accessed from the Connections Navigator. The next image shows the PL/SQL editor interface when using the Connections Navigator to open an existing PL/SQL package body.

```
EMP_PKG          EMP_PKG BODY

  CREATE OR REPLACE
  PACKAGE BODY EMP_PKG IS

  PROCEDURE EMP_proc (v_ename IN varchar2)
  is

  cursor emp_cur is
     select ename, deptno
     from emp;

  v_dname dept.dname%TYPE;

  v_oraerr number(10);
  v_oramsg varchar2(1200);

  BEGIN

  select EMP_pkg.EMP_func(deptno)
  into v_dname
  from emp
  where ename = v_ename;

  dbms_output.put_line('Employee ' || v_ename || ' works in dept ' || v_dname);

  EXCEPTION

  when NO_DATA_FOUND then
     dbms_output.put_line('No Data Found');
     raise;
  when OTHERS then
     v_oraerr := SQLCODE;
```

Editing PL/SQL Code

The Connections Navigator allows easy access to the packages, procedures, functions, and database triggers the user has permission to work with. Figure 7-1 shows a right-click operation on the EMP_ PKG Body, starting a PL/SQL editor interface window with the contents of the package.

Notice the options in the context menu in Figure 7-1. PL/SQL code can be opened into a PL/SQL editor interface window, compiled normally, or compiled for debug. The Compile For Debug option puts special tags into the compiled code as required by the PL/SQL debugger. The PL/SQL compiler can also be signaled with the keystroke combination ctrl-shift-f9. The code can be executed or executed for debug. A PL/SQL profile can be taken of the code.

Figure 7-2 shows the toolbar on the PL/SQL editor interface window. There are similar options on this interface. The buttons from left to right are execute, execute with debugging, compile, and compile for debug.

Compiling PL/SQL Code

PL/SQL code is easily compiled, which also saves it to the Oracle database. The PL/SQL code does not have to be in a code window to be compiled. The compile or compile for debug buttons can be pressed from the PL/SQL editor interface toolbar (see Figure 7-2) or from the Connections Navigator context menu (see Figure 7-1).

PL/SQL code from file systems can be opened. They are initially brought into SQL Developer using the SQL Window interface. Make sure to associate a database connection to this SQL window by using the drop-down menu on the right side of the toolbar to make the toolbar buttons available

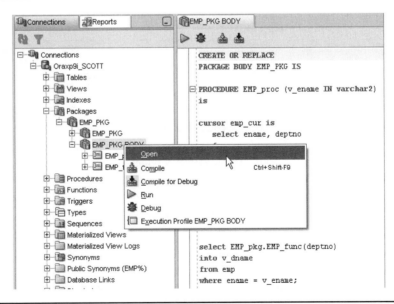

FIGURE 7-1. *Accessing PL/SQL code from the Connections Navigator*

FIGURE 7-2. *Code editor window toolbar*

for use. Execute the code from here; it will be compiled and will then be available from the Connections Navigator.

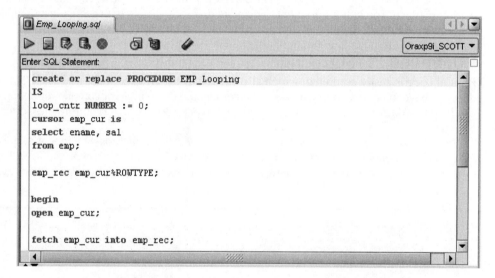

The next image includes the message from the lower-left corner of SQL Developer showing that the code in the SQL window was processed.

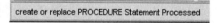

Click the refresh button on the Connections Navigator toolbar (or from the context menu from the connection itself), and the PL/SQL code will appear in the appropriate object category. The next image shows the EMP_Looping procedure object display from the Connections Navigator. Notice the toolbar buttons that include pinning, edit (which will load the procedure into the PL/SQL editor interface), refresh, and Actions—actions include grant, revoke, drop, and compile dependencies.

TIP
PL/SQL packages, procedures, functions, and database trigger code can be saved to your computer's file system by using the Export option discussed in Chapter 8.

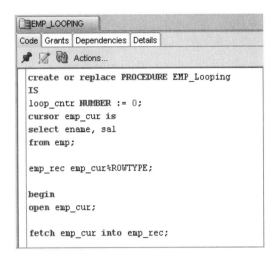

If there are errors in the code, the PL/SQL editor will highlight the line and the error messages will appear in the Log window. Notice the code on line 14 has "FETCH" spelled incorrectly. The compiler highlighted the correct line, and the log shows the actual Oracle error messages generated.

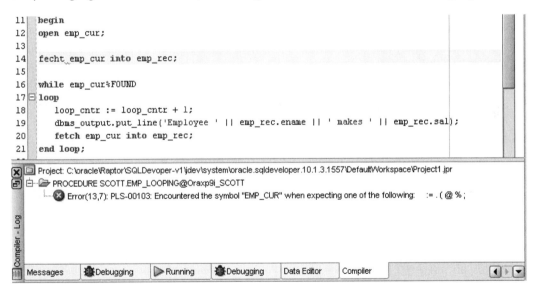

Executing Packages, Procedures, and Functions

PL/SQL code can be executed from the Connections Navigator Object context menu (right-click to get the options in Figure 7-3) by selecting Run.

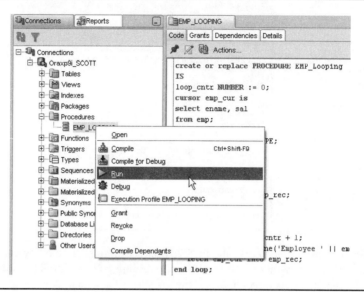

FIGURE 7-3. *Connection Menu object context menu*

This action will start the Run PL/SQL dialog box. The toolbar in the PL/SQL editor interface (refer back to Figure 7-2), will also start this same dialog box. If the PL/SQL code needs any parameters, these can be supplied in this dialog box. Click OK to execute the procedure.

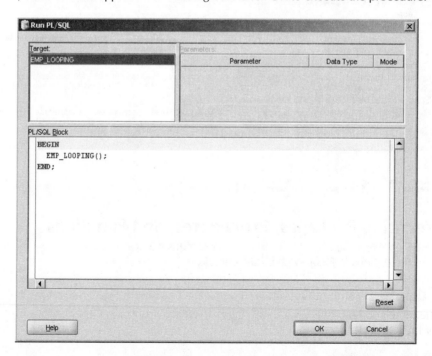

The running log will appear at the bottom of the SQL Developer interface. All of the output will be displayed in the Running tab.

PL/SQL can also be executed from the SQL window interface. Notice the "execute". Execute this statement using the execute script or f5 key. Any output from the PL/SQL execution will be displayed in the Script Output tab.

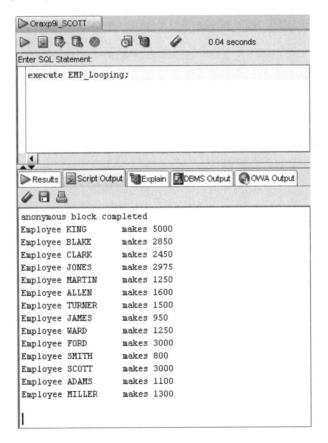

Coding Productivity

The same code snippets and code insights discussed in Chapter 6 for SQL code are also available for PL/SQL code.

Code Snippets

Code snippets are discussed in detail in Chapter 6. All of these features are available in the PL/SQL editor interface as well. The next image shows the PL/SQL Programming Techniques snippets. Drag and drop the snippets of interest into the PL/SQL editor interface and adjust the code as necessary.

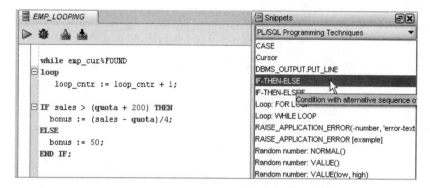

Code Insight

Code insight displays pop-up boxes with either column information or procedure/function options information. Code insights are triggered by a ".". The other code assistant available is code completion insight. This assistant displays available packages and is triggered by CTRL-SPACE.

Code insight is useful to display table columns in a context menu selection or available Oracle package options, again, in a pop-up menu selection. Both types of selections are triggered by entering the table name or the package name followed by a "." and simply waiting a second (this waiting period is an adjustable parameter as discussed in Chapter 4). The image on the left shows the available columns for the DEPT table, and the image on the right shows the available package options for the package DBMS_OUTPUT. Click an entry and hit enter or double-click a column to make your selection.

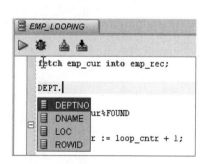

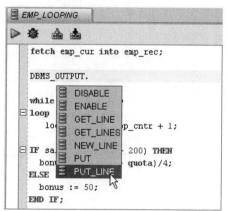

Code completion insight gives a list of available package names. Simply press the keys ctrl-space and a context menu of all available Oracle packages will appear. If a partial string is entered followed by a ctrl-space, all objects with this partial string will be displayed.

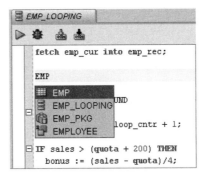

You can see the context menu for the Oracle packages. Scroll through the list to find the package desired. To get the options for these packages, simply press ctrl-space again or use the "." after the package name as just described.

PL/SQL Code Formatting

PL/SQL code can also be formatted using the Format SQL context menu item (right-click in the PL/SQL editor interface window). This image shows the Format SQL option on the context menu, and the image on the next page shows the code formatted after the selection.

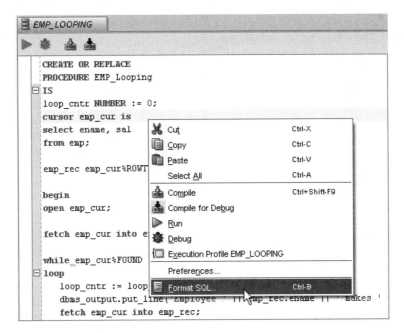

```
EMP_LOOPING

CREATE OR REPLACE PROCEDURE emp_looping IS loop_cntr NUMBER := 0;
CURSOR emp_cur IS
SELECT ename,
  sal
FROM emp;

emp_rec emp_cur % rowtype;

BEGIN

  OPEN emp_cur;

  FETCH emp_cur
  INTO emp_rec;

  WHILE emp_cur % FOUND
  LOOP
    loop_cntr := loop_cntr + 1;
    DBMS_OUTPUT.PUT_LINE('Employee ' || emp_rec.ename || ' makes ' || emp_rec
    FETCH emp_cur
    INTO emp_rec;
  END LOOP;

  CLOSE emp_cur;

END;
```

Using the PL/SQL Debugger

SQL Developer has a complete PL/SQL symbolic debugger. A symbolic debugger allows code to be executed one line at a time and the contents of variables to be visible and changeable. SQL Developer allows for this and much more.

SQL Developer allows the execution of the code to be paused whenever a particular line is hit, or when a particular condition exists (such as when a variable meets a certain condition), by setting breakpoints or conditional breakpoints. This ability to stop the code is called setting breakpoints. A user can even set a breakpoint inside a loop and have it stop processing after so many iterations of the loop are encountered.

SQL Developer also has the ability to monitor variables, using what are called watches. SQL Developer automatically sets up watches on all variables and cursors. The user can see the data as the cursor variables are being fetched. Any watched variable could have its contents changed.

SQL Developer allows code to be executed one line at a time. Called routines can be entered (stepped into) or skipped (stepped over).

A Quick Walkthrough

The next image shows the Compile For Debug button. Before code can be debugged using the debugger, it has to be compiled using this option. This option is also available from the Connections Navigator context menu (refer back to Figure 7-3), as well as from the PL/SQL editor interface context menu (right-click in the PL/SQL editor interface).

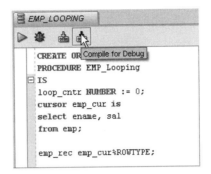

This next image shows the left gutter options of the PL/SQL editor interface window. Breakpoints can be toggled, bookmarks can be toggled (as discussed in Chapter 8), and line numbers can be toggled.

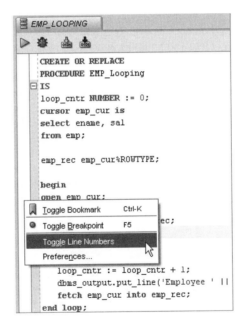

TIP
When debugging, I find the line numbers handy, as several of the views will refer to the watches and breakpoints at certain line numbers.

Breakpoints can be set using the toggle on this display, from the line where the breakpoint is desired. Simply clicking in the gutter next to the line where the breakpoint is desired can also set breakpoints. Breakpoints show up as a red dot, as shown in Figure 7-4.

To start debugging, simply click the debug execute button on the PL/SQL editor interface toolbar (or by selecting Debug from the Connections Navigator or PL/SQL editor interface context

```
13
14   fetch emp_cur into emp_rec;
15   |
16   while emp_cur%FOUND
17 ☐ loop
      loop_cntr := loop_cntr + 1;
18    dbms_output.put_line('Employee ' || emp_rec.ename || '
20    fetch emp_cur into emp_rec;
21   end loop;
22
23   close emp_cur;
24
```

FIGURE 7-4. *Setting breakpoints*

menus) and the call stack, breakpoints, watches, and log tabs will all appear. These windows can be undocked (just like the Help and Snippets windows), closed, and required using the File | View | Debugger menu bar options.

If the routines being debugged have any input parameters, the same PL/SQL parameters window will appear as it would for a normal execution, allowing for the input of parameters.

Notice in Figure 7-5 that debugging has commenced and that the code execution is paused at the breakpoint set just inside the loop from Figure 7-4. The red arrow at line 18 shows the current statement being executed. The breakpoint was hit because the line turned light blue. These breakpoints can be edited and their scope changed; these features are discussed later in this chapter.

There are several menu items, toolbar buttons, and function keys that control the execution and flow of the debugging session. On the debugger toolbar, the buttons from left to right are

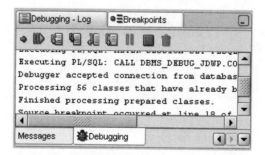

- Find Execution point (jumps the cursor to the current debug statement)
- Resume (or F9 resumes the debugging session)
- Step Over (or F8 is useful for line-at-a-time debugging and to skip over any called functions or other procedures)

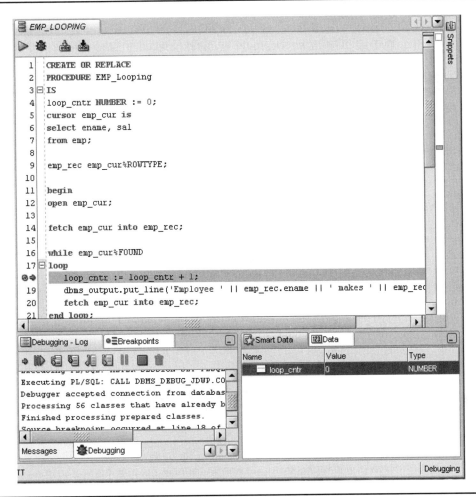

FIGURE 7-5. *Debugging paused at line 18*

- Step Into (or F7 is useful to advance to the next line of code in the main sequence or in a called routine)

- Step Out (or SHIFT-F7 is used to exit a called routine, and Step Into will also exit the routine; either one will then return debugging to the calling routine)

- Pause (pauses the debugging operation)

- Terminate (terminates the routine and the debug session)

- Garbage Collection

The SQL Developer Debug menu item also gives control over the debugging session. Notice there is a bit more functionality here:

- Step To End Of Method (goes to the end and terminates the procedure)
- Continue Step (or SHIFT-F8, functions like Step Into)
- Run To Cursor (or F4, acts like a single-breakpoint stopping operation when the code execution hits the line of code the cursor is sitting on)
- Set Next Statement

Once the routine begins executing in debug mode, several displays with tabs will appear in the PL/SQL editor interface window. These interfaces are used to display important information about the debug session. Each interface is undockable but minimizable, like the Snippets and Help interfaces.

The call stack window shows the current routine that is being debugged. All PL/SQL functions and procedures referenced by this debug session will appear in this window.

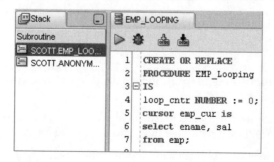

Two data display tabs display just the PL/SQL variables or the PL/SQL variables and the cursor variables. The Smart Data shows all the variables defined in the routine, and the Data tab lists both the defined variables and any cursors. Clicking the "+" next to the cursor will expose all the columns in the cursor. Notice that the data will change as the debug session progresses (i.e., proceeds through the PL/SQL code). The next section will show how the contents of these variables can be modified.

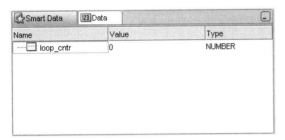 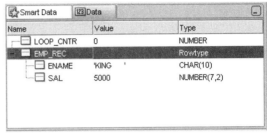

The variable contents are also displayable from the PL/SQL editor interface window. The first image shows the contents of a variable being displayed with a mouse hover, and the second image shows the contents of a cursor being displayed with a mouse hover.

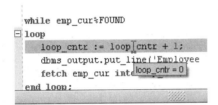 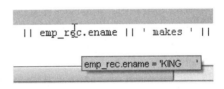

The flow of the debug session really depends on what problem the user is trying to solve within the code.

A simple debug session could entail just leaving the cursor on a line after a point where the contents of certain variables can be examined or changed. Use the Run To Cursor feature to perform this task. The PL/SQL code might be having problems with certain data within a loop. Setting a breakpoint inside the loop will allow for variables to be examined with each loop of the PL/SQL code, and pressing Resume will execute the code until the breakpoint is encountered again (or the next breakpoint is encountered). Some users set a breakpoint early in the code (or use the Run To Cursor feature) and then use the Step Into button (or f7) to walk through the PL/SQL code and called routines one line at a time.

This is a symbolic debugger. It does allow for pausing of code execution, for display of all variables, and for these variables to be changed. This debugger also allows for breakpoints to stop execution of the code. The next section will show how to set conditions on these breakpoints so that they stop the code execution after so many loops or when a variable contains a certain value.

Tools like this make finding problems in PL/SQL code a snap.

Setting Breakpoints

The Breakpoint tab (see the image on the next page) shows all the breakpoints that have been currently set and at which line number they were set. Notice the highlighted breakpoint next. This is the breakpoint that was set with a mouse click in the gutter in Figure 7-5.

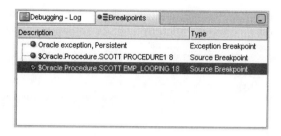

Right-clicking this breakpoint will pop up a context menu of options. Notice that particular breakpoints can be disabled or deleted, and that all breakpoints can be enabled, disabled, or deleted at once. The breakpoints can be exported and saved to use in future debug sessions of this particular PL/SQL routine. Preferences can be set from here as well.

The Edit option brings up the Edit Breakpoint dialog box, which shows some useful information, lets you set conditions on when the breakpoint will stop the code, and provides for grouping breakpoints.

The Conditions tab of the breakpoint dialog allows the breakpoint to stop execution when a variable meets a certain condition (when LINE_CNTR = 20 or ENAME = 'HARPER', for example). Notice the Pass Count option. This allows a breakpoint to be put inside a loop and to stop code after the breakpoint has been encountered the number of times given. Enabling either of these features will make this a "conditional breakpoint."

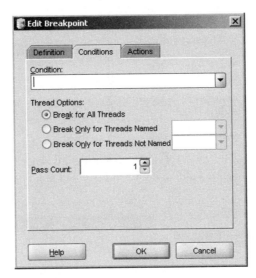

The next image shows the final tab of the Edit Breakpoint dialog box. Here you state what action is desired when the breakpoint is encountered. Most of the time, the desired behavior is to halt code execution. Notice that any established breakpoint groups can be enabled or disabled from this tab as well.

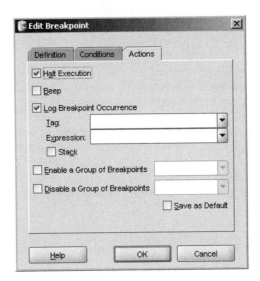

Monitoring or Changing Data

When the debugging session commences, the Smart Data tab will be populated with the various PL/SQL variables defined in the declaration section of the code, and the Data tab will contain the same variables as well as the cursor variables.

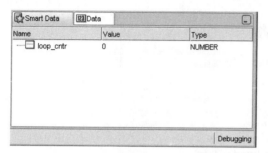 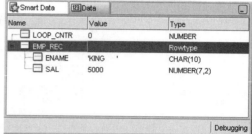

Right-click to access the Watch Context menu options. These options may change depending on the data type. The Modify Value option will open a dialog box allowing the variable contents to be modified.

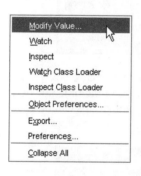 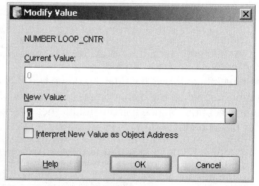

The Watch option will open another tab (called Watch) allowing this variable to appear in its own undockable tab. Additional options in this tab provide for pinning, inspection of the object type class, etc. The Inspect option allows the variable's class information to be displayed. The Watch Class Loader and Inspect Class Loader options give additional information about the type classes for this variable. The Object Preferences afford control over how the contents of the variable are displayed in this watch. Export allows the contents of the selected data item to be exported. The Preferences option accesses the SQL Developer Debug preferences dialog box. The Collapse All option closes this data display interface.

Use the SQL Developer View | Debugger menu option to reopen any of the debugging session information display panels.

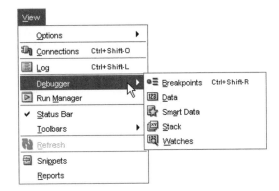

Remote Debugging

SQL Developer allows for the debug process to be initiated from a user session! This is a powerful feature that starts the debugging process in SQL Developer when a user process accesses the PL/SQL code being debugged. This type of debugging captures the user's data in a real-time environment.

NOTE
Make sure to compile the desired PL/SQL code for Debug and place a breakpoint in the code where desired when the code is initiated by the user session.

The first step is to select Remote Debug from the connection context menu (right-click the user connection). This brings up the Debugger – Listen for JPDA dialog box. The debug port range is typically 4000–4999 (and is configurable via Tools | Preferences | Debugger on the SQL Developer menu bar). Notice in the image on the right that the run manager is indicating that this debugging session is listening for input.

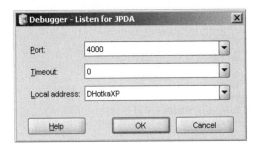 

Now the user needs to tell the Oracle debugger that it wants to pass debug information to the selected port. Do this with the following command, which also includes the call to the EMP_FUNC package:

```
SQL> execute DBMS_DEBUG_JDWP.CONNECT_TCP('192.75.1.21',4000);
SQL> select EMP_PKG.EMP_FUNC(10) from DUAL;
```

The next image shows the SQL Developer with the EMP_FUNC compiled for debug, a breakpoint at line 47, and the fact that the breakpoint has been reached by the debugger. Notice the variable contains the data passed from the user session. At this point, the user session is waiting for the code to execute.

```
37  FUNCTION EMP_func (v_DEPTNO NUMBER)
38  return varchar2
39  is
40
41  v_dname dept.dname%TYPE;
42
43  v_oraerr number(10);
44  v_oramsg varchar2(1200);
45
46  begin
    select dname
48  into v_dname
49  from dept
50  where v_deptno = deptno;
51  return(v_dname);
52              v_deptno = 10
53  EXCEPTION
```

Remote Debug is now providing for real-time code debugging.

Using the Debugging Environment
This is a robust symbolic debugger. It can be used in a number of methods, depending on the nature of the problem encountered within the PL/SQL code environment.

The PL/SQL code has to first be compiled for debug, as shown here. This option tells the PL/SQL compiler to put the necessary debug tag information inside the compiled PL/SQL code. All the PL/SQL codes dependencies will be compiled for debug. This may take some time if there are quite a number of called routines from the selected PL/SQL code.

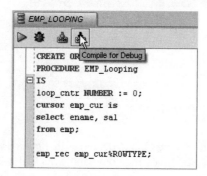

```
EMP_LOOPING

CREATE OR Compile for Debug
PROCEDURE EMP_Looping
IS
loop_cntr NUMBER := 0;
cursor emp_cur is
select ename, sal
from emp;

emp_rec emp_cur%ROWTYPE;
```

To walk through the code from beginning to end, set a breakpoint at the first executable line and then use the f7 key or Step Into button to walk through the PL/SQL code and called routines one line at a time.

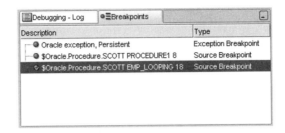

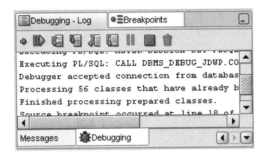

Hover the cursor over any variable to quickly view its current value.

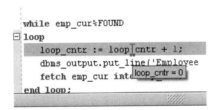

Breakpoints can be set inside of loops. After compiling for debug, find the line where code execution is to be paused and click in the gutter or click the line of code and press f5 to set a breakpoint. When the code is executed for debug, this line will turn blue when the selected line is encountered and code processing will be suspended. Variables can be inspected and their values changed if necessary.

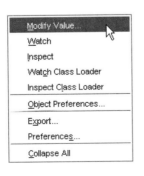

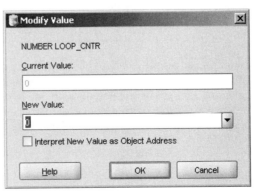

To resume code processing, press the Step Into or Step Over to walk through the code one line at a time from this breakpoint, or else click Resume button or press f9 and code execution will continue until another breakpoint is encountered or the end of the routine is executed.

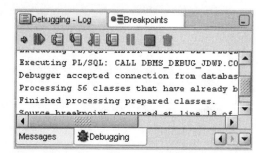

Breakpoints can be set inside of loops and their pass count can be set so that code is suspended once the breakpoint has been encountered by the debug session the number of times indicated by the pass count. This feature is nice when the PL/SQL code loops a routine 500 times and then seems to have issues from this point on. Using a breakpoint with a pass count of 499 will allow for code execution until the code is on its last loop through this particular routine of interest. Then the Step Into button can be used to walk through each line of code from this point forward.

Breakpoints can also be set here based on the contents of a variable. This allows for the code to be paused when a particular data item is encountered, again, allowing for the variables to be interrogated and code to be stepped through one line at a time.

The Debugger toolbar or the Debugging menu items are useful to control the flow of execution. Notice that a function key is associated with just about any debugging function.

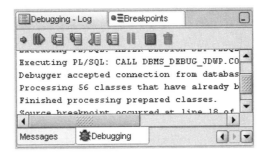

The debugging session can be terminated by using the Terminate button on the Debugging tab or by right-clicking the debug session in the Run Manager window and selecting Terminate from the context menu.

If SQL Developer is closed with an active PL/SQL execution or debug session still running, a dialog box will appear asking to terminate the executing processes.

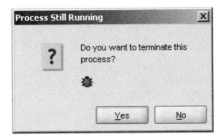

Summary

The goal of this chapter is to illustrate how easy it is to work with PL/SQL packages, procedures, and functions using SQL Developer. Topics covered include creating template PL/SQL packages, procedures, and functions, editing the code, working with the productivity enhancers (code snippets and code insights), and using the PL/SQL debugger.

CHAPTER
8

Additional Topics

QL Developer has several features that just didn't seem to fit in any of the other chapters. This chapter will cover how to find and replace code items, how to use bookmarks to quickly navigate around larger code sets, and how to create DDL scripts of any database object or group of database objects.

Find and Replace Text

SQL Developer has the same find/replace text that is found in most development and word-processing tools. SQL Developer also has a find feature that highlights all the occurrences of a string as well.

Using Find and Replace Features

The menu sequence Edit | Find or the CTRL-F key sequence will start the Find Text dialog box, as shown here. The usual options are present. Notice that the Replace With check box can be selected and replacement text entered. The Find Next (F3) key or the Find Previous (SHIFT-F3) key combination will highlight the next or previous text as indicted by the Text To Search For box. When this text is selected, click Replace or press CTRL-R and the text in the Replace With box will be substituted for the highlighted text from the Find operation.

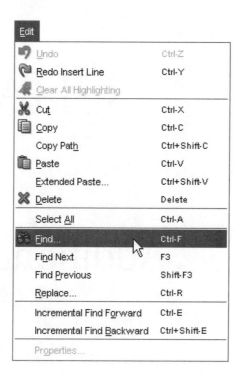

The image that follows on the left shows the Replace With text box filled out and the Scope set to Prompted. This will bring up a Replace Text box (on the right) that will walk through all the Text To Search For and prompt to replace the text with the Replace With text.

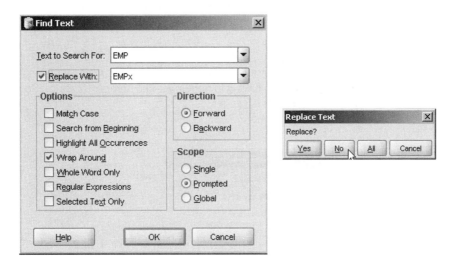

NOTE
The Find and Replace features illustrated work in both the PL/SQL Code Editor and the SQL worksheet interfaces.

Using Incremental Find Forward/Backward

The Incremental Find Forward/Backward option allows text to be searched for and highlighted wherever it appears throughout the code. This feature is activated from the Edit | Incremental Find

Forward (from the position of the cursor) or Backward (from the position of the cursor) item from the SQL Developer menu bar or by using CTRL-E or CTRL-SHIFT-E (for backward).

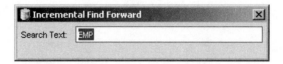

Notice in the next image that as "EMP" is entered into the Search Text dialog box, the EMP code is highlighted throughout the visible code (at line numbers 2, 4, 7, and 18). This text search is not case sensitive.

Quickly Navigating Around Code

The SQL worksheet and PL/SQL Code window interfaces have visible line numbers, allow for bookmarks (tags that appear in a pop-up menu for easy navigation to bookmarked items), and allow you to go to a particular line number.

Using Bookmarks

SQL Developer allows for tags to be inserted into code at the user's choice for easy navigation to this point in the code in the future without having to remember line number locations. Bookmarks are set by a right-click on the code interface's left gutter.

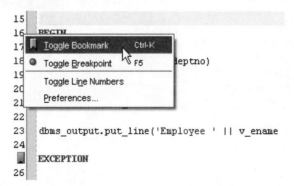

The next image shows the SQL Developer Navigate | Toggle Bookmark or Go To Bookmark menu. A CTRL-K key sequence will also set a bookmark on the same line as the cursor.

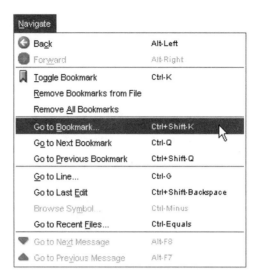

The Go To Bookmark menu choice (or the CTRL-SHIFT-K key sequence) will bring up the Go To Bookmark dialog box. Simply double-click a listed bookmark and the location will be centered in the particular interface window and the cursor placed on the first position of the line.

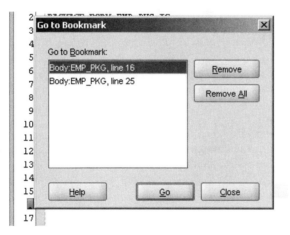

Using Line Numbers

Line numbers are available by right-clicking in either interface on the left gutter and selecting Toggle Line Numbers. The toggle turns items off that are on and on that are off.

The SQL Developer menu item Navigate | Go To Line Number opens the Go To Line Number dialog box and will adjust the display to show this line and position the cursor to the first position of the line.

Database Export

Using SQL Developer, you can export DDL syntax for all database objects to a file. First, choose Tools | Export from the SQL Developer menu bar.

TIP
I use this interface to create the DDL necessary to create a test environment for the application I am currently testing.

Notice in the Export dialog box that the File box is for the filename and location. The Browse button next to this box can be used to navigate to the target folder for this file. The Options area gives control over the options associated with the syntax, the appearance of the syntax, and various options of some of the output:

- The Storage option will include the storage clauses on all data-oriented objects being exported.
- The Terminator option will put a line terminator at the end of each line.
- Pretty Print will format each DDL statement in the output.
- Include BYTE Keyword will include the BYTE syntax when appropriate.
- Add Force To Views will add this syntax if view objects are exported.
- Constraints As Alters will apply any constraint requested as an alter statement to the object rather than as an in-line constraint.

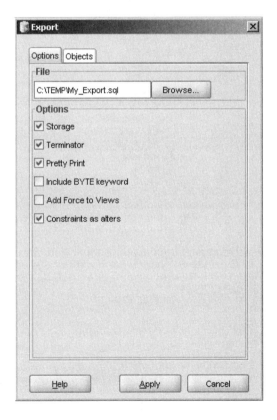

NOTE

This feature uses DBMS_METADATA, and the dialog boxes simply pass parameters to this package. The objects do appear in the output file alphabetically by object type (e.g., tables are almost last in the output). It is a planned enhancement to create a script that will be ready to execute (e.g., objects will be in the proper order for creation).

The Objects tab allows you to select the objects that are to be exported. The Apply button will execute the request and create the appropriate DDL as requested in the output file.

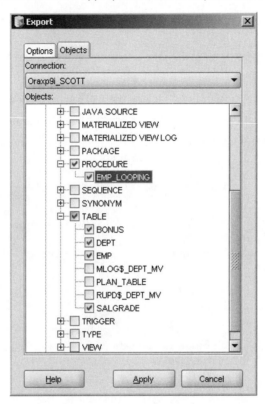

Here is a sample of the output from the options specified in the preceding two images:

```
REM SCOTT EMP

  CREATE TABLE "SCOTT"."EMP"
   (    "EMPNO" NUMBER(4,0) NOT NULL ENABLE,
        "ENAME" CHAR(10),
        "JOB" CHAR(9),
        "MGR" NUMBER(4,0),
        "HIREDATE" DATE,
        "SAL" NUMBER(7,2),
        "COMM" NUMBER(7,2),
        "DEPTNO" NUMBER(2,0) NOT NULL ENABLE
   ) PCTFREE 10 PCTUSED 40 INITRANS 1 MAXTRANS 255 NOCOMPRESS LOGGING
  STORAGE(INITIAL 65536 NEXT 1048576 MINEXTENTS 1 MAXEXTENTS 2147483645
  PCTINCREASE 0 FREELISTS 1 FREELIST GROUPS 1 BUFFER_POOL DEFAULT)
  TABLESPACE "USERS" ;
  CREATE UNIQUE INDEX "SCOTT"."EMP_PRIMARY_KEY" ON "SCOTT"."EMP" ("EMPNO")
  PCTFREE 10 INITRANS 2 MAXTRANS 255
  STORAGE(INITIAL 65536 NEXT 1048576 MINEXTENTS 1 MAXEXTENTS 2147483645
  PCTINCREASE 0 FREELISTS 1 FREELIST GROUPS 1 BUFFER_POOL DEFAULT)
  TABLESPACE "USERS" ;
  ALTER TABLE "SCOTT"."EMP" ADD CONSTRAINT "EMP_PRIMARY_KEY" PRIMARY KEY ("EMPNO")
  USING INDEX PCTFREE 10 INITRANS 2 MAXTRANS 255
  STORAGE(INITIAL 65536 NEXT 1048576 MINEXTENTS 1 MAXEXTENTS 2147483645
  PCTINCREASE 0 FREELISTS 1 FREELIST GROUPS 1 BUFFER_POOL DEFAULT)
  TABLESPACE "USERS" ENABLE;
  ALTER TABLE "SCOTT"."EMP" ADD CONSTRAINT "EMP_SELF_KEY" FOREIGN KEY ("MGR")
          REFERENCES "SCOTT"."EMP" ("EMPNO") ENABLE;
  ALTER TABLE "SCOTT"."EMP" ADD CONSTRAINT "EMP_FOREIGN_KEY" FOREIGN KEY ("DEPTNO")
          REFERENCES "SCOTT"."DEPT" ("DEPTNO") ENABLE;
```

Summary

The goal of this chapter is to cover some remaining SQL Developer features that should help increase your productivity with both SQL Developer and the Oracle RDBMS. This chapter covered finding code strings, replacing code strings, using bookmarks and line numbers to quickly navigate around larger code sets, and using the Export feature, which allows DDL scripts to be made from literally any object in the database.

PART

III

SQL Developer Reports

CHAPTER
9

Available Reports

QL Developer comes with many reports that provide a plethora of information to the user. These predefined reports contain information about the Oracle instance and its objects. The reports can be accessed without a database connection and will prompt for a database connection when being executed. Many of the reports will prompt the user for information required to run the report. The SQL behind the reports is easily accessed and can be changed and run in a SQL Worksheet window as well. The next image shows the Reports Navigation window and the major report categories. Many of these report categories have subcategories. These categories are used to organize the reports to help the user find the report of interest. Chapter 10 will illustrate how users can add their own reports to this Report Navigation interface.

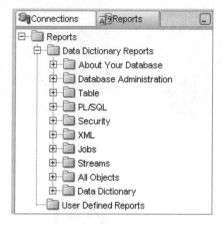

This chapter will discuss all the reports currently available in SQL Developer.

 NOTE
SQL Developer uses the data dictionary views for these reports. There are four major categories for these views: ones that start with V$ (usually requires DBA privileges), DBA_ views (you would need DBA privileges to view the contents), USER_ views (you need to be the owner of the object to see the contents), and ALL_ views (any user can see the contents of these views). Some reports may not work due to your current database access privileges.

Running Reports

Reports are executed by double-clicking the report desired in the Reports Navigation window. Simply navigate through the Reports Navigator hierarchy and double-click to execute or right-mouse click to access the context menu.

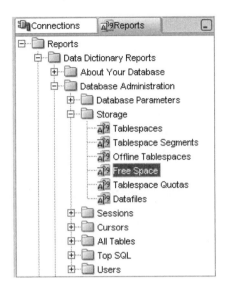

NOTE

The Free Space and All Tables reports are shown in this section to demonstrate report functionality. Both reports will be covered in detail later in this chapter.

All reports require a database connection, some reports require additional information, and most of the reports have optional parameters. If a database connection has not been established with the Reports Navigation window, the user will be prompted for a database connection. A new connection can also be created from this interface. See Chapter 2 for details on how to fill out this connection dialog box. The next image shows the connection request information when the Storage | Free Space report is selected.

TIP
Using the Connections box in the upper-right corner of the report interface will allow this same report to be run on other instances of Oracle.

The Storage Free Space report has an optional parameter (bind variable). This particular report will show all available free space for all tablespaces in the connected instance (check the Null box), or just the free space for a particular tablespace (enter a valid tablespace name). Once the selection is made, click Apply to execute the report; the results will be displayed in a Report View interface.

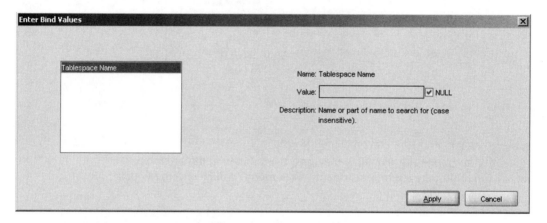

NOTE
Some of the reports require DBA privileges (i.e., the report is based on a DBA_ view). You may or may not be able to run a report, depending on your user privileges.

Figure 9-1 on the next page shows the report execution results in a Report View interface. This interface allows the user to move and resize the columns, save the output data, and load it into a SQL Worksheet window. Notice that the toolbar allows for the report view to be pinned (Freeze View), executed again (if there are input variables, the Enter Bind Values box just shown will reappear), or the report can be loaded into a SQL Worksheet window. The database connection can be changed on the right side of the report view interface.

The next image shows the context menu (right-click the data area of the Report view). The data can be saved in a variety of formats in the same fashion as the other data grid interfaces.

Free Space					◀▶▼

					Oraxp9i_SCOTT ▼

Tablespace	Allocated MB	Used MB	Free MB	Used	Data Files
CWMLITE	20	9.375	10.625	0.46875	1
DRSYS	20	9.6875	10.3125	0.484375	1
EXAMPLE	198.75	148.6875	50.0625	0.748113207547169811320754716981...	2
INDX	25	0.0625	24.9375	0.0025	1
ODM	20	9.3125	10.6875	0.465625	1
SYSTEM	600	417.875	182.125	0.696458333333333333333333333333...	2
TOOLS	597.8125	196.5	401.3125	0.328698379508625196027182435 96...	3
UNDOTBS1	460	10.5625	449.4375	0.0229619565217391304347826086 9...	1
USERS	508.75	430	78.75	0.845208845208845208845208845 20...	3
XDB	38.125	37.9375	0.1875	0.995081967213114754098360655 73...	1

FIGURE 9-1.   *Storage free space report*

These reports can also be executed from a context menu started from the Reports Navigator. The options include

- **Open**   Runs the report, prompts for any input variables, and reuses an un-pinned Report View window, or opens a new window.

- **Open New Window**   Runs the report, prompts for any input variables, and opens a new Report View window for the results.

- **Show Properties**   Displays the SQL statement assigned to the report. This SQL can be copied and pasted into a SQL worksheet.

- **Copy**   Copies the Report definition to the computer's clipboard.

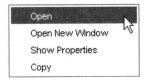

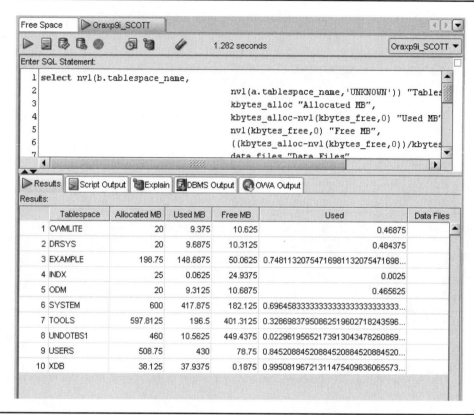

FIGURE 9-2. *The free space report SQL executed in the SQL Worksheet window*

Clicking the SQL Worksheet button on the Report View toolbar (refer back to Figure 9-1) will open a SQL Worksheet window and load the report's SQL text into this window. Figure 9-2 shows the results of clicking this SQL Worksheet button and then executing the Free Space SQL in the SQL worksheet.

TIP
This allows you to modify and execute the SQL for this report and even save it to a user-defined report for future use. User-defined reports are covered in Chapter 10.

Drillable Reports

SQL Developer allows for most of the supported object types to be drilled on (i.e., by double-clicking) to show the object definition interface. The first image that follows shows the All Tables report. Double-clicking the EMP table name in this report brings up the table definition screen for the EMP table.

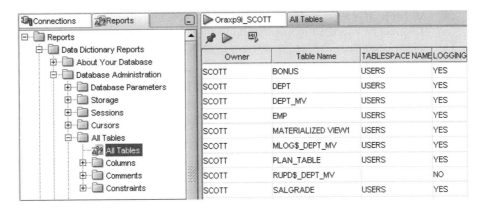

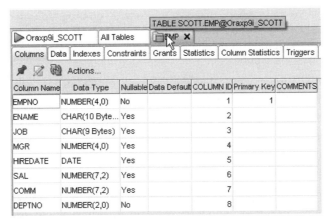

Data Dictionary Reports

SQL Developer has the following major report categories:

- About Your Database contains two reports showing the version of the Oracle instance and the database's National Language Support.

- Database Administration contains the following subcategories, each of which contains specific reports to the subcategory:

  - Database Parameters has two reports showing all the database parameters and nondefault database parameters.

  - Storage includes a series of reports about the tablespaces, which include free space, quotas, assigned data files, and total sizes.

  - Sessions includes a series of reports on session counts, session information, sessions organized by module and by users, and active/inactive/background/system session information.

  - Cursors have two reports that show the open cursors by session and cursor detail.

- All Tables has a variety of subcategories that contain reports on tables in the database instance, including table information, table columns, comments, constraints, indexes, triggers, statistics, storage parameters, organization, and quality assurance (referential integrity information).

- Top SQL contains five reports full of useful information to help identify poorly performing SQL.

- Users contains a variety of reports showing user account information, locked accounts, expired accounts, counts on a variety of account types, and more.

- Table has a variety of subcategories that contain reports on the database connection's user tables, including table information, table columns, comments, constraints, indexes, triggers, statistics, storage parameters, organization, and quality assurance (referential integrity information).

- PL/SQL has three reports that give information on program unit parameters, program unit line counts, and a report that will search PL/SQL source code for specific text strings (such as a column name, table name, or procedure name) and report on all objects where this string appears.

- Security has several subcategories that contain reports on grants and privileges, auditing, encrypted columns, and database policies.

- XML contains a single report of XML schemas.

- Jobs has three reports that show the connected user's scheduled jobs, all jobs, and DBA jobs.

- Streams has two reports showing the connected user's stream rules and all stream rules.

- All Objects has several reports showing all objects, invalid objects, collection types, dependencies (shows various database relationships), public synonyms, and public database links.

- Data Dictionary has two reports that list the V$ tables and the V$ table columns.

The remainder of this chapter will illustrate each of these reports and discuss their high points.

About Your Database

There are two reports in this category. The first image that follows displays the Oracle instance banner information. The second shows the current settings for the national language support features.

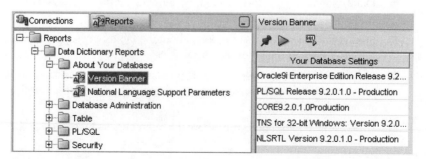

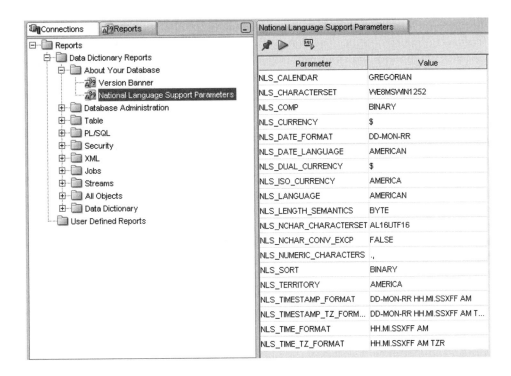

Database Administration

The Database Administration reports are organized into seven categories that allow users to quickly find the type of information they are searching for.

Database Parameters

The Database Parameters category has two reports: the All Parameters report and the Non-Default Parameters report. Both reports have a parameter that will help the user limit the output to just the parameters that match a particular parameter name. The All Parameters report shows all the database parameters and their current settings. The Non-Default Parameters report displays the same columns, displaying only those parameters not set to their default settings. All of the columns on these reports are from the V$Parameter data dictionary view.

Both reports contain these columns:

- ■ Parameter Name
- ■ Type (field data type)
- ■ Value (current setting)
- ■ Default (default setting)
- ■ Session Modifiable (can the session alter this value real time?)
- ■ System Modifiable (can this parameter be changed real time?)
- ■ Description (brief description of the parameter)

Storage

The Storage category contains six reports that report on a variety of information about the Oracle instance's tablespace. These reports include information about the values and settings used when the tablespace was created, remaining free space, and information about the data files assigned to the tablespace.

Each of these reports has an optional tablespace name parameter.

The Tablespace report shows useful information about tablespaces, their unit of extent allocation, their current status, their default block size, and the space management options that are currently assigned. Information for this report comes from the DBA_TABLESPACES table. The report columns include

- Tablespace
- Block Size
- Initial Extent
- Next Extent
- Minimum Extents
- Maximum Extents
- Percent Increase
- Minimum Extent Length
- Status (online or offline)
- Contents (permanent or temporary)
- Logging (changed blocks being archived)
- Force Logging
- Extent Management (local or dictionary)
- Allocation Type
- Plugged In
- Segment Space Management

See the Database Administration Guide for details on the various options available for Tablespaces.

The Tablespace Segments report shows the data-oriented objects (tables, indexes, materialized views, etc.) and the number of assigned extents and their current storage space in the database (extents times extent size from the Tablespace report). This information comes from the DBA_ SEGMENTS table. The columns include

- Owner
- Tablespace
- Segment (database object name)
- Extents
- Megabytes (extents times extent size)

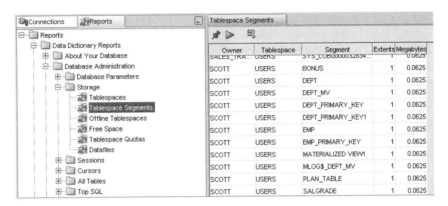

Notice in this image that the SCOTT database objects are displayed.

TIP
This might be a good report to run in the SQL Worksheet window and add a WHERE clause condition to select the extent information for the user of interest. This report can take a while to execute.

The Offline Tablespace report shows the offline status of a particular tablespace (via the input parameter) or the offline status of any tablespace. There are only two columns in this report: the tablespace name and the current status of the tablespace. This information comes from the DBA_TABLESPACES report and is a subset of the Tablespace Segments report just shown.

The Free Space report shows useful information about how much space is both used in a tablespace and is currently available. The report columns include

- Tablespace
- Allocated MB (total space allocated in megabytes)
- Used MB (total space currently consumed in megabytes)
- Free MB (total space currently available in megabytes)
- Used (a percentage of the used space versus the total space available)
- Data Files (number of assigned data files)

The information in this report comes from DBA_FREE_SPACE and DBA_DATA_FILES.

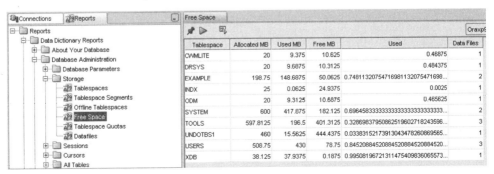

TIP
*I find this report of particular interest for my general Oracle space
management needs. I can quickly see if any of my tablespaces are
about to run out of space, or I can check this report before doing a
sizable data load to make sure there is room for the new data.*

The Tablespace Quotas report shows the tablespaces and users with assigned quotas, their
current tablespace space usage, and their quota assignments. The report columns include

- Tablespace Name
- Username
- Megabytes (current storage allocation)
- Max Megabytes (maximum allocation assigned to this user)
- Quota (current quota allocation)

This information comes from the table DBA_TS_QUOTAS.

The Datafiles report shows useful information about the physical data files that are assigned to
the tablespace. This report includes the following information:

- Tablespace
- Filename (with full path)
- Size MB (current size of the file in megabytes)
- Maximum Size MB (maximum size in megabytes)
- Autoextensible (can this tablespace automatically grow if needed?)

This information comes from DBA_DATA_FILES.

TIP
*If you need to see the assigned database file numbers, load the SQL
for this report into the SQL worksheet and add the column FILE_ID.
This information might be useful if you are trying to track down a file
corruption error or are doing database block dumps, etc.*

Sessions
The Sessions category contains nine reports that detail a variety of information as it relates to
various Oracle sessions for the connected instance of Oracle.

The Sessions Count by Status report (active, inactive, background, etc.) contains the columns

- Status
- Distinct OS Users
- Type
- Count

This information comes from the V$Sessions database virtual table.

The Sessions Count by OS User report displays similar information and is probably more useful for reporting on an instance of Oracle hosted on a Unix-based system than on the PC-hosted Oracle instance that these examples were created on. There are two columns: OS User and Count. This information is queried from the V$Sessions database virtual table.

The Sessions report shows details about the active user sessions. This report contains these columns:

- Session ID
- Username
- Seconds in Wait
- Command (type of SQL being executed)
- Machine
- OS User
- Status (active or inactive on this report)
- Module (usually the program executing the SQL shows up here). SCOTT is the user for the SQL Developer session.
- Action
- Resource Consumer Group
- Client Information
- Client Identifier

This information comes from the V$Sessions database virtual table.

The Sessions by Module report is a subset and summary of the detailed module information from the Sessions report. It might be useful to know how many sessions are using the same program. There are only two columns: Module and Session Count. This information comes from the V$Sessions database virtual table.

The Sessions by Username report is also a summary report from the detailed Sessions report. This report has two columns: Username and Session Count. This might be useful to know how many different sessions each user is using.

The Active Sessions report and the Inactive Sessions report are subsets of the information from the Sessions report. These two reports also have the same columns. The only difference is the data displayed is organized by the Status column (active vs. inactive).

The Oracle RDBMS has both background processes and processes being executed by the SYSTEM account. The final two reports display this information from the V$Session table.

NOTE
There is a type column in the V$Session table. The contents of this column are either USER or BACKGROUND. The SYSTEM reports key off the OSUser column with a value of 'SYSTEM'.

Cursors

SQL Developer allows for users to see how many active SQL statements each user is processing. Cursors are the work area assigned to SQL statements in the Process Global Area (PGA) of the Oracle instance. The Cursors by Session report shows how many cursor areas each user has. The columns available in this report are SID (session identifier) Username, and a count of the Open Cursors. This information is queried from the V$Open_Cursors and V$Sessions database virtual tables.

The Cursor Detail report shown next shows the current SQL statement, or the most current SQL statement processed by the cursor. This report has a parameter for SID (session identifier). If no parameter is given, the system and dictionary SQL will also be displayed (i.e., the SQL that Oracle uses for SQL syntax checking, permissions, etc.). Columns in this report include

- Saddr (session address)

- SID (session identifier)

- User Name

- Address (pointer to the current SQL in V$SQL database virtual table)

- Hash Value (another pointer to the current SQL in V$SQL database virtual table)

- SQL Text (current SQL statement)

Information on this report comes from the V$Open_Cursors database virtual table.

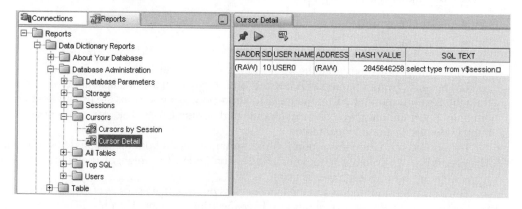

TIP
I use the Sessions report to see which user I want to investigate further. I use the Session ID from that report as a parameter in this report to see exactly what the user of interest is currently executing. It is easy to find useful information in one report and supporting detail in another report using SQL Developer.

All Tables

The All Tables category has one report, the All Tables report, and nine subcategories of other related reports. This category reports on tables, columns, referential integrity, storage information, statistics, indexes, and more.

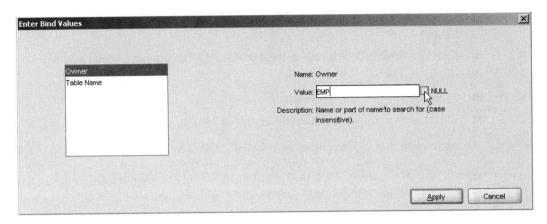

The All Tables report is used to show a variety of information and statistics about all tables in the Oracle instance (a rather sizeable report), or for tables belonging to a particular user, or tables that have a particular name, or both.

This report has two optional input variables. Both parameters can be left blank with the NULL box checked. The parameters are also a string search. The preceding report shows the output when the Owner parameter is left NULL and the Table Name is populated with 'EMP'.

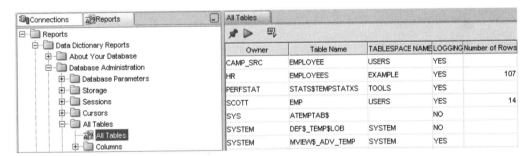

Notice in the All Tables report shown previously that any table with the string 'EMP' is returned along with useful information. This report is useful to see tables by table name or by particular users, the tablespaces the tables are assigned to, and some cost-based statistical information (if this information has been collected). Columns in this report include

- Owner (user name)
- Table Name
- Tablespace Name
- Logging (are changes to this object being logged for recovery?)
- Number of Rows
- Blocks (number of blocks assigned to the object)
- Empty Blocks
- Average Row Length

- Cached (is this object always loaded into cache when accessed?—a storage parameter setting)

- Date Last Analyzed (best way to tell if cost-based statistics have been collected)

- Last Analyzed

- Partitioned (is this table partitioned?)

- IOT Type (is this table an Indexed-Organized Table?)

The information in this table comes from the ALL_TABLES dictionary table.

TIP
Double-clicking any of these table names will bring up that object's definition interface.

The Columns subcategory has two reports: the Columns report and the Datatype Occurrence report. Both reports have three optional input variables: User, Table Name, and Column Name. These reports can be rather sizable if no input variables are used.

The Columns report shows the column name and basic information about the column. This report includes these columns:

- Owner
- Table Name
- Column Name
- Column Type (along with precision as specified when the table was created or altered)
- Nullable (can this column contain null values?)

This report is useful if a user is either looking to see if a column name exists in the database, or if a user is going to change the specs of a particular column.

The information in this report comes from the DBA_TAB_COLUMNS data dictionary view.

The Datatype Occurrences report is useful to show the various datatypes assigned to columns throughout the database, for a particular user, for a particular table, or for a particular column name. The report columns include Owner, Type (datatype with precision), and Occurrences (a count of the times it occurs associated to the report parameters used).

The information in this report also comes from the DBA_TAB_COLUMNS data dictionary view. This report might be useful to make sure that certain columns have a consistent datatype.

The Comments subcategory has four reports. The first three reports (All Table Comments, Tables with Comments, and Tables without Comments) report on comments defined at the table level, and all have two optional parameters (User and Table Name).

The All Table Comments report shows comments at the table level. Columns in this report include

- Owner
- Table Name
- Table Type
- Comments

The information in this report comes from the DBA_TAB_COMMENTS data dictionary view.

The Tables with Comments report is a subset of the All Table Comments report showing just the tables that have comments on them. The report columns and the source of the information are the same as in the All Table Comments report.

The Tables without Comments report is a subset of the All Table Comments report showing just the tables that do not have comments on them. The report columns (except there is no need for a Comments column here) and the source of the information are the same as in the All Table Comments report.

The Column Comments report shows comments defined at the column level. This report has one additional optional input parameter of 'Column Name'. Columns on this report include

- Owner
- Table Name
- Column Name
- Comments

Information on this report comes from the data dictionary views DBA_TAB_COMMENTS and DBA_COL_COMMENTS.

The Constraints subcategory has seven reports that display information on all kinds of constraints, organizing the available data by all constraints, enabled and disabled constraints, then a report on each major type of constraint (primary key, unique, foreign key, and check constraints). Each of these reports has two optional parameters: Owner and Table Name.

The All Constraints report shows all the defined constraints across the database (no parameters) or the defined constraints by user, or by table name, or both. The All Constraints report has these columns of information:

- Owner
- Table Name
- Constraint Name
- Constraint Type
- Status (enabled or disabled)

This information comes from the DBA_CONSTRAINTS data dictionary view.

The next two reports, Enabled Constraints and Disabled Constraints, are both subsets of the All Constraints reports. They have all the same columns except for the column the report is based on, as this information now becomes part of the selection criteria for the report.

The remaining four reports in this category give additional details as noted for each of the constraint types.

The Primary Key Constraints report has an additional column showing the columns that the key values are established on. Information for this report comes from the DBA_CONSTRAINTS, DBA_INDEXES, and DBA_IND_COLUMNS data dictionary views.

The Unique Constraints report also has an additional column showing the key column information. This report gets its information from the same sources as the Primary Key Constraints report.

The Foreign Key Constraints report has additional information showing the objects and columns the listed foreign keys point to. This report contains the columns

- Owner
- Table Name
- Constraint Name
- Delete Rule
- Columns
- Owner of Related Table
- Related Table
- Related Constraint

This information comes from the following sources: DBA_CONSTRAINTS and DBA_CONS_COLUMNS data dictionary views.

The Check Constraints report lists the constraint information along with the Owner, Table Name, Constraint Name, and Status. This information comes from the DBA_CONSTRAINTS data dictionary view.

The Index subcategory has four reports. Only the All Indexes report has two optional parameters: Owner and Table Name.

The All Index report is useful to see the indexes, types of indexes, and related table information. This report includes the columns

- Owner
- Index Name
- Index Type (Normal is a B-tree index; other types include Bitmap, Function-Based, IOT, set)
- Table Owner
- Table Name
- Uniqueness

This information comes from the DBA_INDEXES data dictionary view.

The Indexes by Type report shows the different types and number of indexes by this type across the connected database instance. Columns include Index Type and Index Count. This information also comes from the DBA_INDEXES data dictionary view.

The Indexes by Status report shows the valid versus nonvalid indexes across the connected database instance. Columns include Status and Index Count. This information comes from the DBA_INDEXES data dictionary view.

The Unusable Indexes report shows indexes with the status of 'UNUSABLE'. Columns on this report will help find the unusable index and associated table. Columns on this report include

- Owner
- Index Name

- Index Type
- Table Name

Information on this report comes from the DBA_INDEXES data dictionary view.

The Triggers subcategory contains four reports: All Triggers, Enabled Triggers, Disabled Triggers, and Trigger Summary. The Enabled Triggers and Disabled Triggers reports are subsets of the All Triggers report and are only missing the Status column, as this has become a selection criterion for these subset reports.

The first three reports have optional parameters of Owner and Table Name, and the Trigger Summary report has only the Owner optional parameter.

The information for all of these reports in this category comes from the DBA_TRIGGERS data dictionary view.

The All Triggers, Enabled Triggers, and Disabled Triggers reports have these columns of information:

- Owner
- Trigger Name
- Trigger Type
- Table Owner
- Table Name
- Column Name
- Triggering Event
- Status (only appears on the All Tables report)

The Trigger Summary report displays counts of the various types of triggers across the database (no input parameters) or by Owner. The columns of information include

- Owner
- Trigger Count
- Table Count
- Number Enabled
- Number Disabled

The Statistics subcategory has three reports: Statistics, Most Rows, and Largest Average Row Length. The latter two reports are subsets of the Statistics report and have the data sorted in descending order based on the report title.

Columns in these reports include

- Owner
- Table Name
- Last Analyzed
- Rows

- Average Row Length
- Table Type

Information for these reports comes from DBA_TABLES.

The Storage subcategory has two reports: Tables by Tablespace and Table Count by Tablespace. Both of these reports have a single optional Owner parameter.

The Tables by Tablespace report includes

- Table Name
- Tablespace
- Megabytes (size in bytes of the object in the tablespace)

Information for this report comes from the USER_SEGMENTS data dictionary view.

TIP
I find the Tables by Tablespace report particularly useful when looking at tables to move to other tablespaces. It is helpful to know what other objects are also in the tablespaces.

The Table Count by Tablespace report shows the number of tables per tablespace and their size in bytes. This report includes the columns

- Tablespace
- Tables (a count of the tables by tablespace)
- Megabytes (a sum of the size of the tables in the tablespace)
- Max Megabytes
- Quota

The information for this report comes from the USER_SEGMENTS data dictionary view.

The Organization subcategory contains three subcategories, and this version of SQL Developer has a single report in each one. These reports will show Partitioned tables, Clustered objects tables, and Index Organized tables. There are no input parameters with any of these reports.

The Partitioned Table report shows the tables across the connected database instance that are partitioned, who owns them, and other useful information. This report contains the columns

- Owner
- Table Name
- Tablespace Name
- Logging
- Partitioned

This information comes from the DBA_TABLES data dictionary view.

The Clusters report shows the tables across the connected database instance that are clustered, who owns them, and other useful information. This report contains the Owner, Cluster Name, and Tablespace Name columns. This information comes from the DBA_CLUSTERS data dictionary view.

The Index Organized Table report shows the index-organized tables across the connected database instance. This report contains the columns

- Owner
- Table Name
- Tablespace Name
- Logging
- Partitioned
- IOT Name

This information comes from the DBA_TABLES data dictionary view.

The Quality Assurance subcategory has three reports that display tables without primary keys, tables without indexes, and tables with unindexed foreign keys. These reports have one optional input parameter for Owner.

The Tables without Primary Keys report contains the columns Owner and Table name. This information comes from the DBA_TABLES and DBA_CONSTRAINTS data dictionary views.

The Tables without Indexes report has the Owner and Table Name columns, and this information comes from the data dictionary views DBA_TABLES and DBA_INDEXES.

The Tables with Unindexed Foreign Keys report has the following columns:

- Owner
- Table Name
- Constraint Name
- Foreign Key Column 1
- Foreign Key Column 2

This information comes from the DBA_CONS_COLUMNS and the DBA_CONSTRAINTS data dictionary views.

TIP
*I run this report before application implementation to make sure I
have all the foreign keys indexed. Loading this report's SQL into the
SQL worksheet, one can easily make this a "SQL Creating SQL" script
that will then create the missing indexes.*

Top SQL
The Top SQL category helps the user identify poorly performing SQL. There are five reports in this category, and they all contain the same information; the descending sort order is indicated by the report title.

NOTE
Since the information displayed in these reports is identical except for sort order, it will be discussed only once in this section as a group.

The next image shows the Top SQL by CPU. The other reports in this category are

■ Top SQL by Disk Reads (physical reads)

■ Top SQL by Buffer Gets (logical reads)

■ Top SQL by Executions (number of times executed)

■ Top SQL by Buffer Gets/Rows Processed (logical rows read divided by rows returned)

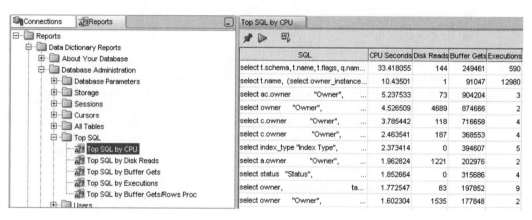

These reports contain the columns

■ SQL (the SQL text)

■ CPU Seconds

■ Disk Reads

■ Buffer Gets

■ Executions

■ Buffer gets/rows proc

■ Buffer gets/executions (percentage of logical reads divided by the number of executions)

■ Elapsed Seconds (wall clock time)

■ Module (program that issued the SQL statement)

This information comes from the V$SQL virtual database table.

Users

The Users category contains eleven reports that display useful information about the various user accounts for the connected database instance.

The All Users report shows a variety of information about the user accounts themselves. This report has the columns

- Username
- Created
- Account Status
- Lock Date
- Expiration Date
- Default Tablespace
- Temporary Tablespace
- Profile
- Initial RSRC Consumer Group
- External Name

This information comes from the DBA_USERS data dictionary view.

The Recently Created report lists the connected database instance's user accounts in descending order from when they were created. Notice there are various Account Statuses visible in this report. The columns of this report include

- Username
- Created
- Days Ago
- Account Status
- External Name

This information comes from the DBA_USERS data dictionary view.

The Count by Profile report shows all the different profiles set up for users and how many users are assigned to each one. This report only has two columns: Profile and User Count. This information also comes from the DBA_USERS data dictionary view.

The Count by Default Tablespace report shows the default tablespaces assigned to various users and how many users are assigned to each tablespace. This report has two columns as well: Default Tablespace and User Count. This information also comes from the DBA_USERS data dictionary view.

The Temporary Tablespace report shows the various temporary tablespaces and the number of users assigned to each one. This report has two columns of information: Temporary Tablespace and User Count. This information comes from the DBA_USERS data dictionary view.

TIP
If your application does a lot of sorting, and most of the users are assigned to a single temporary tablespace, then there might be performance gains by creating additional temporary tablespaces and editing the users so that the users are evenly divided across the various temporary tablespaces.

The Object Count by Type shows the various object types by user. There are three columns of information: Owner, Object Type, and Object Count. This information comes from the DBA_ OBJECTS data dictionary view.

The Locked Users and the Expired Users reports are subsets of the All Users report. The columns are the same as the All Users report. The Locked Users report shows the users with accounts that have been locked by the administrator, and the Expired Users report shows the users whose accounts have expired.

The last two reports are Users with Objects and Users without Objects. The Users with Objects report has two columns of information: Owner and Object Count. The Users without Objects only lists the Owners. This information comes from the DBA_OBJECTS data dictionary view.

Table

The Table category of reports is for the SQL Developer's connected user's tables and information. All the reports are identical to those discussed in the All Tables section under Database Administration. The main difference between these reports and the Database Administration reports is that these reports are based on the USER_ dictionary views (any user can run these reports) rather than the DBA_ dictionary views the Database Administration reports are based on (users would need DBA privileges). The other difference is that the User Name or Owner is not part of any optional parameter, as this information is part of the selection criteria for this series of reports.

The only new report in this section is the User Synonym report. This report shows the synonyms owned by the connected user's account and contains the following information:

- Name
- Object Owner
- Object Name
- Database Link
- Object Type

This information is queried from the USER_SYNONYMS and the ALL_OBJECTS data dictionary views.

PL/SQL

The PL/SQL category contains three reports that display a variety of useful information about the PL/SQL code, including listing in/out variables, source-code line counts, and text search of the PL/SQL code.

The Program Unit Arguments shows all the procedures and packages owned by the connected user and their in/out variables. The following information is available:

- Owner
- Package
- Program Unit
- Position (position of the variable in the code unit)
- In Out (what type of variable is it)

This information is queried from the ALL_ARGUMENTS data dictionary view.

The Unit Line Counts report shows the various program units, their types, and the code module line counts. This report contains the following information:

■ Owner

■ Object Type

■ PL/SQL Object Name

■ Lines

This information comes from ALL_SOURCE data dictionary view.

The Search Source Code report allows for the searching of text strings in the connected user's source code. This report has two optional input variables: Owner and Text Search. The report shown here left the Owner at its NULL default setting and searched for the text string 'EMP'. This report shows:

■ Owner

■ PL/SQL Object Name

■ Type

■ Line (where the text string was found)

■ Text (line of code containing the text string)

This information is queried from the ALL_SOURCE data dictionary view.

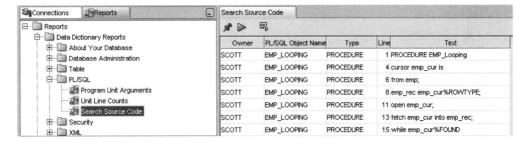

TIP

This report would be very useful to also search across the database for particular strings, such as column names that were being changed. Simply copy the report SQL to the SQL worksheet (click the SQL Worksheet button on the report toolbar) and remove the where clause condition 'owner = user'.

Security

The Security category has five subcategories that help to organize the related reports, making the topics of interest easier to find. The subcategories are

■ Grants and Privileges

■ Public Grants

- Auditing
- Encryption
- Policies

These reports show grant and privilege information as they relate to the connected user.

The Grants and Privileges subcategory has four reports. These reports are organized by Object Grants, Column Privileges, Role Privileges, and System Privileges.

The Object Grants report shows the Owner (Grantor) and to whom this user has granted access privileges. The columns of information include

- Grantor (who is doing the granting)
- Grantee (the recipient of the grant)
- Table Name
- Privilege
- Grantable

This information comes from the ALL_TAB_PRIVS data dictionary view.

The Column Privileges report has similar information as the Objects Grants with the addition of the Column Name column. This report will display any column-level privileges granted. This information comes from the ALL_COLS_PRIVS data dictionary view.

The Role Privileges report shows the roles granted to the connected user. The columns of information include

- User
- Granted Role
- Admin Option
- Default Role

This information comes from the USER_ROLE_PRIVS data dictionary view.

The System Privileges report shows the system-level privileges granted to the connected user. The columns include Privilege and Admin Option (this user is able to pass the privilege on to other users). This information comes from the USER_SYS_PRIVS data dictionary view.

The Public Grants subcategory has six reports:

- All Grants
- Grant SELECT
- Grant DML
- Grant EXECUTE
- Grantable
- Counts by Grantor

The first report, All Grants, is the all-inclusive report that shows the grantor, the grantee, information relating to the object, and the type of privilege being shared. The next four reports are subsets of this All Grants report highlighting the grant information featured by the report title. The last report shows the number of grants per grantor.

The column information for the first five reports is the same and includes

- Grantor (user ID doing the granting)
- Grantee (PUBLIC in this series of reports)
- Table Schema (recipient user ID of the grant)
- Table Name
- Privilege
- Grantable
- Hierarchy

This information for this series of reports comes from the ALL_TAB_PRIVS data dictionary view.

The Auditing subcategory has only one report: the Audit Policies. This report illustrates any audit policies for the connected instance of Oracle. The columns on this report include

- Object Schema
- Object Name
- Policy Name
- Policy Text
- Policy Column
- PF Schema
- PF Package
- PF Function
- Enabled

This information comes from the ALL_AUDIT_POLICIES data dictionary view.

XML

The XML category has only one report, the XML Schemas report. This report shows column information that includes

- Owner
- Schema URL
- Local
- Schema
- Qual Schema URL

This information is queried from the ALL_XML_SCHEMAS data dictionary view.

Jobs

The Jobs category reports on information in the DBMS_JOBS Oracle-based scheduling system. Each of these reports has the same columns, which include

- Job
- Log User
- Privilege User
- Schema User
- Last Date
- This Date
- Next Date
- Total Time
- Broken
- Interval
- Failures
- What

This information comes from the USER_JOBS data dictionary view.

Streams

The Streams category has two reports: Your Stream Rules and All Stream Rules. These reports have the same column information:

- Streams Name
- Rule Set Owner
- Rule Set Name
- Rule Owner
- Rule Name
- Rule Condition
- Rule Set Type
- Streams Rules
- Schema Name
- Object Name
- Subsetting Operation
- DML Condition
- Rule Type

This information comes from the ALL_STREAMS_RULES data dictionary view.

All Objects

The All Objects category contains seven reports that illustrate the database objects, collection types, object dependences, synonyms, and database links.

The All Object report is used to show the various objects, their status, and some useful statistics. This report has two optional parameters: Owner and Object Name. The report has the following column information:

- Owner
- Object Type
- Object Name
- Status
- Date Created
- Last DDL

This information is queried from the ALL_OBJECTS data dictionary view.

The Invalid Objects report shows any object with a status other than Valid. This report has only the Owner as an optional parameter. This report has three columns: Owner, Object Type, and Object Name. This information also comes from the ALL_OBJECTS data dictionary view.

The Object Count by Type report shows the distinct object types and a count for each type. There is only one optional parameter for the Owner column. This report has three columns: Owner, Object Type, and Object Count.

The Collection Types report shows the various data collections structures across the connected database instance or for the Owner (optional parameter). The columns in this report include

- Owner
- Type Name
- Collection Type
- Upper Bound
- Element Type Modifier
- Element Type Owner
- Element Type Name
- Length
- Precision
- Scale
- Character Set

This information comes from the ALL_COLL_TYPES data dictionary view.

The Dependencies report shows all the various relationships for the database objects for the entire connected instance or for the Owner (single optional parameter). This report has the following columns:

- Owner
- Name
- Type
- Referenced Owner
- Referenced Name
- Referenced Type
- Referenced Link Name
- Dependency Type

This information comes from the ALL_DEPENDENCIES data dictionary view.

The Public Synonyms report shows all the public synonyms and the underlying objects they point to. This report can also be used to look up partial string references using the optional input parameter. This feature would be very handy in trying to find the right data dictionary view. The report contains the following columns:

- Name
- Object Owner
- Object Name
- Database Link
- Object Type

This information is in the ALL_SYNONYMS data dictionary view.

The Public Database Links report is used to show all public database links across the connected instance of Oracle. There is also a string search optional parameter. The columns include

- Name
- User Name
- Host
- Created

This information comes from the ALL_DB_LINKS data dictionary view.

Data Dictionary

The final category shows information about the data dictionary views available for the connected instance of Oracle. The first report, Dictionary Views, has two columns: Data Dictionary View Name and Comments. This report should be helpful in finding certain types of information in the Oracle data dictionary.

Dictionary Views	
Data Dictionary View Name	Comments
ALL_ALL_TABLES	Description of all object and relational t...
ALL_APPLY	Details about each apply process that ...
ALL_APPLY_CONFLICT_COLUMNS	Details about conflict resolution on tabl...
ALL_APPLY_DML_HANDLERS	Details about the dml handler on tables ...
ALL_APPLY_ERROR	Error transactions that were generate...
ALL_APPLY_KEY_COLUMNS	Alternative key columns for a STREAM...
ALL_APPLY_PARAMETERS	Details about parameters of each appl...
ALL_APPLY_PROGRESS	Information about the progress made b...
ALL_ARGUMENTS	Arguments in object accessible to the ...
ALL_ASSOCIATIONS	All associations available to the user
ALL_AUDIT_POLICIES	All fine grained auditing policies in the ...

TIP
Load the SQL from this report into the SQL window interface and perform a LIKE search on keywords on the Comments column to find specific data dictionary view names.

The Dictionary View Columns report illustrates all the columns with comments for each of the data dictionary views. The next image shows the columns, which include Data Dictionary View Name, Column Name, and Comments. This information comes from the ALL_OBJECTS, ALL_TAB_COLUMNS, and ALL_COL_COMMENTS data dictionary views.

Dictionary View Columns		
Data Dictionary View Name	Column Name	Comments
ALL_ALL_TABLES	OWNER	Owner of the table
ALL_ALL_TABLES	TABLE_NAME	Name of the table
ALL_ALL_TABLES	TABLESPACE_NAME	Name of the tablespace containing the ...
ALL_ALL_TABLES	CLUSTER_NAME	Name of the cluster, if any, to which th...
ALL_ALL_TABLES	IOT_NAME	Name of the index-only table, if any, to ...
ALL_ALL_TABLES	PCT_FREE	Minimum percentage of free space in a...
ALL_ALL_TABLES	PCT_USED	Minimum percentage of used space in ...
ALL_ALL_TABLES	INI_TRANS	Initial number of transactions
ALL_ALL_TABLES	MAX_TRANS	Maximum number of transactions
ALL_ALL_TABLES	INITIAL_EXTENT	Size of the initial extent in bytes
ALL_ALL_TABLES	NEXT_EXTENT	Size of secondary extents in bytes
ALL_ALL_TABLES	MIN_EXTENTS	Minimum number of extents allowed in ...
ALL_ALL_TABLES	MAX_EXTENTS	Maximum number of extents allowed in...

TIP
This report has an optional Dictionary View Name, and it is probably best to use the Dictionary Views report described in this section to retrieve the name of the view and use that view name as a parameter in this report to see all the columns and column descriptions for that particular view.

Summary

This chapter outlined the features and benefits of the predefined reports that come with SQL Developer. These reports make it easy to get a variety of information about the Oracle instance. This information includes database instance information, all kinds of object information, storage information, tuning information, and even information from the Oracle dictionary V$ tables, with the proper database privileges. SQL Developer has its own report interface, or the SQL for the reports can be loaded into the SQL worksheet for manipulation and execution. Chapter 10 will show how to save this manipulated SQL to its own new SQL Developer report.

CHAPTER
10

User-Defined Reports

QL Developer allows for reports to be added to the Reports Navigator. These reports can be existing SQL statements from various scripts or from SQL statements adjusted from the existing reports. These user-defined reports allow the user to easily organize and access various SQL statements. This chapter will illustrate how to add categories and how to add reports.

TIP
This is a powerful feature that allows you to take any of your existing SQL reports, organize them, and be able to launch them against any Oracle instance that has been defined to SQL Developer.

These user-defined reports are saved in the C:\Documents and Settings\<user>\.sqldeveloper folder in a file named UserReports.xml. This file will be preserved between SQL Developer upgrades and can also be shared with other users.

TIP
Users sometimes edit this UserReports.xml file and change the report prompts.

Adding Categories

Categories, or folders, are a convenient and easy way to organize reports in SQL Developer. Folders can be nested so that categories can have subcategories as needed for clarity. The next image shows how right-clicking the category displays the context menu for the User Defined Report category.

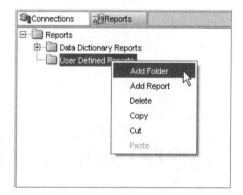

Selecting Add Folder from this context menu opens the Create Folder dialog box. Notice the name is the only required field. Click Apply to create the folder.

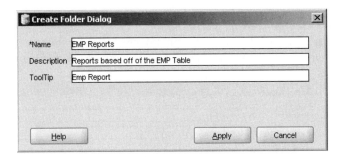

To add subcategories, simply right-click this new category (or folder) to create a folder that would then appear under this folder.

The Edit option will now appear when accessing the context menu from a created category. This Edit option will redisplay the same information as illustrated in the preceding image and allow for any change to any of the information.

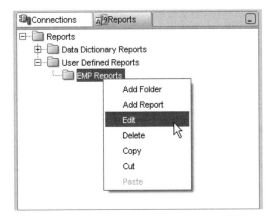

Notice the context menu also allows the folder to be deleted, copied, or cut.

The tooltip pop-up entered in the Create Folder dialog appears when the mouse is hovered over the new folder.

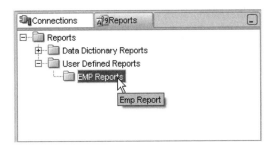

Adding Reports

Adding reports is easy using the context menu from the category the report is to be associated with. Select Add Report from the context menu just shown and the Create Report dialog box will appear.

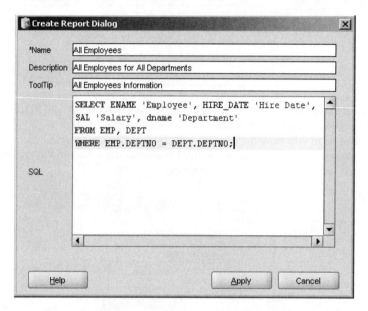

SQL Developer will complain of any syntax errors with a pop-up box. Simply select Edit Report from the context menu to return to the dialog box to fix any issues or to add additional requirements to the report.

The report generated from the Create Report dialog appears next. Also notice that the tooltip appears as well.

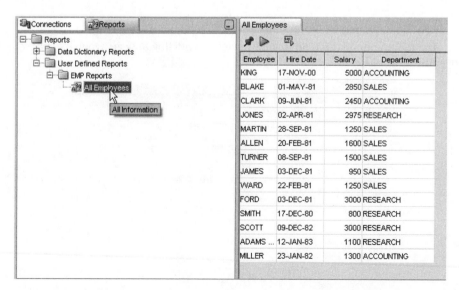

TIP
This interface allows you to add any customized report modified from the existing set of reports that came with SQL Developer.

Reports with Optional Input Variables

User-defined reports can easily have the same optional parameters as seen in the dictionary reports in Chapter 9.

TIP
I simply selected Copy from the context menu on the All Employees report and selected Paste from the context menu on the same category. I then simply edited the copied report, changing the title, description, and tooltip, along with adding the additional required SQL code.

Notice the SQL in the Edit Report dialog box shown next. The SQL has been coded so that the :DEPTNO is included and that the :DEPTNO is also checked for NULL values. This coding technique allows the SQL to produce the correct results whether a parameter was supplied or not.

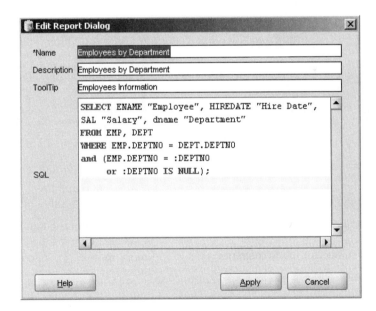

The next image shows the Enter Bind Values dialog box, where we enter the value for DEPTNO. Notice that the bind variable name appeared. This text can be up to thirty positions long, so there is room to make a rather descriptive message for the bind variable.

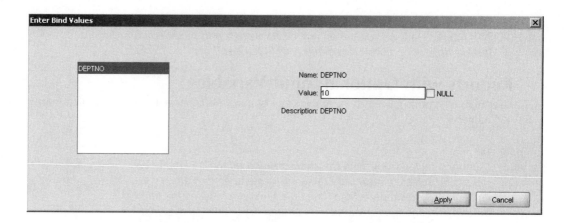

NOTE
The bind variables will appear in the Enter Bind Values box in the
order that they appear in the SQL text.

The next image shows the resulting report.

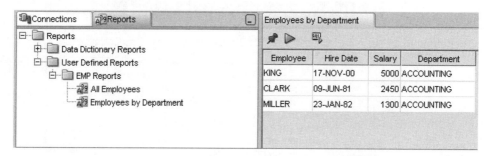

Summary

This chapter illustrated how to create SQL Developer reports from existing SQL statements. SQL Developer also allows for additional categories to be added, allowing the user to organize these reports into folders for future reference.

PART
IV

Appendixes

APPENDIX
A

Feature, Function, and
Keystroke Cross-Reference

QL Developer has over fifty different keystroke combinations. Some of the keystrokes are context sensitive (i.e., the same keystroke in different interfaces is assigned to different functions). SQL Developer calls these keystrokes "accelerators," and they are modifiable through the Preferences interface. This appendix will list all the default keystrokes in order both by keystroke and again by their features and functions.

Keystroke Cross-Reference

Table A-1 shows the available SQL Developer keystrokes and the feature or function they are assigned.

SQL Developer Keystroke	Feature/Function
ALT-F4	Exit
ALT-F7	Go To Previous Message
ALT-F8	Go To Next Message
ALT-LEFT ARROW	Back
ALT-RIGHT ARROW	Forward
CTRL-'-'	Browse Symbol
CTRL-/	Toggle Line Comments
CTRL-=	Go To Recent Files
CTRL-A	Select All
CTRL-ALT-SPACE	Smart Completion Insight
CTRL-B	Format SQL
CTRL-C	Copy
CTRL-D	Clear
CTRL-E	Incremental Find Forward
CTRL-F	Find
CTRL-F4	Close
CTRL-G	Go To Line
CTRL-K	Toggle Bookmark
CTRL-N	New
CTRL-O	Open
CTRL-P	Print
CTRL-Q	Go To Next Bookmark
CTRL-Q	Cancel

TABLE A-1. *SQL Developer Keystroke Cross-Reference*

SQL Developer Keystroke	Feature/Function
CTRL-R	Replace
CTRL-S	Save
CTRL-SHIFT-BACKSPACE	Go to Last Edit
CTRL-SHIFT-C	Copy Path
CTRL-SHIFT-E	Incremental Find Backward
CTRL-SHIFT-F4	Close All
CTRL-SHIFT-K	Go To Bookmark
CTRL-SHIFT-L	Log Window
CTRL-SHIFT-O	Connections Navigator
CTRL-SHIFT-Q	Go To Previous Bookmark
CTRL-SHIFT-SPACE	Parameter Insight
CTRL-SHIFT-V	Extended Paste
CTRL-SPACE	Completion Insight
CTRL-V	Paste
CTRL-X	Cut
CTRL-Y	Redo
CTRL-Z	Undo
DELETE	Delete
F2	Commit
F3	Find Next or Rollback
F5	Toggle Breakpoint
F5	Run as Script
F6	Execute Explain Plan
F7	Step Into
F8 (Debugger)	Step Over
F8 (SQL Worksheet)	SQL History
F9 (Debugger)	Resume Debugging
F9 (SQL Worksheet)	Execute Statement
SHIFT-F3	Find Previous
SHIFT-F7	Step Out
SHIFT-F8	Continue Step

TABLE A-1. *SQL Developer Keystroke Cross-Reference (continued)*

Feature/Function Cross-Reference

Table A-2 illustrates the various SQL Developer features and functions and the keystrokes assigned to them.

SQL Developer Feature/Function	Keystroke
Back	ALT-LEFT ARROW
Browse Symbol	CTRL-'-'
Cancel	CTRL-Q
Clear	CTRL-D
Close	CTRL-F4
Close All	CTRL-SHIFT-F4
Completion Insight	CTRL-SPACE
Commit	F2
Connections Navigator	CTRL-SHIFT-O
Continue Step	SHIFT-F8
Copy	CTRL-C
Copy Path	CTRL-SHIFT-C
Cut	CTRL-X
Delete	DELETE
Execute Explain Plan	F6
Execute Statement	F9 (SQL Worksheet)
Exit	ALT-F4
Extended Paste	CTRL-SHIFT-V
Find	CTRL-F
Find Next	F3
Find Previous	SHIFT-F3
Format SQL	CTRL-B
Forward	ALT-RIGHT ARROW
Go To Bookmark	CTRL-SHIFT-K
Go to Last Edit	CTRL-SHIFT-BACKSPACE
Go To Line	CTRL-G
Go To Next Bookmark	CTRL-Q
Go To Next Message	ALT-F8

TABLE A-2. *Feature/Function Cross-Reference*

SQL Developer Feature/Function	Keystroke
Go To Previous Bookmark	CTRL-SHIFT-Q
Go To Previous Message	ALT-F7
Go To Recent Files	CTRL-=
Incremental Find Backward	CTRL-SHIFT-E
Incremental Find Forward	CTRL-E
Log Window	CTRL-SHIFT-L
New	CTRL-N
Open	CTRL-O
Parameter Insight	CTRL-SHIFT-SPACE
Paste	CTRL-V
Print	CTRL-P
Redo	CTRL-Y
Replace	CTRL-R
Resume Debugging	F9 (Debugger)
Rollback	F3
Run as Script	F5
Save	CTRL-S
Select All	CTRL-A
Smart Completion Insight	CTRL-ALT-SPACE
SQL History	F8 (SQL Worksheet)
Step Into	F7
Step Out	SHIFT-F7
Step Over	F8 (Debugger)
Toggle Bookmark	CTRL-K
Toggle Breakpoint	F5
Toggle Line Comments	CTRL-/
Undo	CTRL-Z

TABLE A-2. *Feature/Function Cross-Reference (continued)*

Summary

This appendix illustrated the keystroke and feature/function assignments in order by both keystroke and again by feature/function.

APPENDIX B

SQL Developer Version 1.1 and Beyond

he next release of SQL Developer was already in the works during the writing of this book. The SQL Developer home web page (http://www.oracle.com/ technology/products/database/sql_developer/index.html) contains a link to the new features being incorporated into the next release or two of SQL Developer. This appendix will discuss several of the major improvements planned for SQL Developer Version 1.1, which is due out in the second half of calendar year 2006.

SQL Developer Version 1.1

Oracle has added a considerable number of features across the product. This appendix will outline many of these improvements. Please read the release notes for each version of SQL Developer for the most current information on new features for the particular release. This appendix used information from the Statement of Direction information on the SQL Developer home page and observations of early releases of SQL Developer Version 1.1. This appendix will discuss many of the intended features but is not a complete list of all enhancements.

TIP
If you have suggestions or ideas for SQL Developer, please participate in the SQL Developer Forum (accessed from the SQL Developer home page).

General Interface Improvements

Oracle has added these features to SQL Developer:

- Additional object and object name filtering features
- Additional object and text search capabilities
- Possibly a schema compare

Object Navigator Improvements

The Object Navigator now supports these newer features:

- Provision for import from Excel spreadsheets in the Table Information data grid
- A single-row viewer for the Table Information data grid
- XML schemas
- Use of F4 key for Table and Object describes
- Times Ten object navigation and SQL worksheet support

SQL Worksheet Improvements

The SQL worksheet now has these new features:

- Highlighting for explain plan lines
- Support for autotrace
- Additional SQL statement formatting

- Xquery
- Snippet management (allows snippets to be easily added and changed)

Data Grid Improvements

The data grid now has sortable fields.

PL/SQL Code Editor Improvements

The PL/SQL code editor has additional editing support, offers improved parsing, and can work with file-based PL/SQL code.

Reports Improvements

The Reports Navigator has several new reports that include Master/Detail data reports. Users will have the ability to query this data and kill user sessions (with proper permissions). The reports also will have charting capabilities as well as additional right-click options. There will be additional drill-down links to other related data as well.

SQL Developer Version 1.2

Oracle is planning on these improvements for SQL Developer Version 1.2. This release is planned for the first half of calendar year 2007. This release will have some useful tuning features that will include

- Access to the PL/SQL Profiler
- An interface to Oracle trace files
- Database activity reporting
- SQL Tuner and Access Advisor

This release will support these additional database objects:

- Tablespace
- Jobs
- Intermedia
- ConText support

Other features planned for this release include

- PDF output
- Version control
- Visual Query Builder
- Oracle 11g database features

Index

GET YOUR **FREE SUBSCRIPTION**
TO ORACLE MAGAZINE

Oracle Magazine is essential gear for today's information technology professionals. Stay informed and increase your productivity with every issue of *Oracle Magazine*. Inside each free bimonthly issue you'll get:

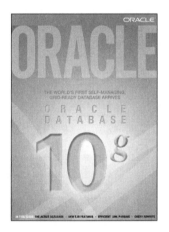

IF THERE ARE OTHER ORACLE USERS AT YOUR LOCATION WHO WOULD LIKE TO RECEIVE THEIR OWN SUBSCRIPTION TO ORACLE MAGAZINE, PLEASE PHOTOCOPY THIS FORM AND PASS IT ALONG.

- Up-to-date information on Oracle Database, Oracle Application Server, Web development, enterprise grid computing, database technology, and business trends
- Third-party vendor news and announcements
- Technical articles on Oracle and partner products, technologies, and operating environments
- Development and administration tips
- Real-world customer stories

Three easy ways to subscribe:

① Web
Visit our Web site at otn.oracle.com/oraclemagazine. You'll find a subscription form there, plus much more!

② Fax
Complete the questionnaire on the back of this card and fax the questionnaire side only to +1.847.763.9638.

③ Mail
Complete the questionnaire on the back of this card and mail it to P.O. Box 1263, Skokie, IL 60076-8263

ORACLE

FREE SUBSCRIPTION

○ **Yes, please send me a FREE subscription to *Oracle Magazine*.** ○ NO
To receive a free subscription to *Oracle Magazine*, you must fill out the entire card, sign it, and date it (incomplete cards cannot be processed or acknowledged). You can also fax your application to +1.847.763.9638.
Or subscribe at our Web site at otn.oracle.com/oraclemagazine

○ From time to time, Oracle Publishing allows our partners exclusive access to our e-mail addresses for special promotions and announcements. To be included in this program, please check this circle.

○ Oracle Publishing allows sharing of our mailing list with selected third parties. If you prefer your mailing address not to be included in this program, please check here. If at any time you would like to be removed from this mailing list, please contact Customer Service at +1.847.647.9630 or send an e-mail to oracle@halldata.com.

signature (required)   date

X

name   title

company   e-mail address

street/p.o. box

city/state/zip or postal code   telephone

country   fax

YOU MUST ANSWER ALL TEN QUESTIONS BELOW.

① WHAT IS THE PRIMARY BUSINESS ACTIVITY OF YOUR FIRM AT THIS LOCATION? (check one only)
- □ 01 Aerospace and Defense Manufacturing
- □ 02 Application Service Provider
- □ 03 Automotive Manufacturing
- □ 04 Chemicals, Oil and Gas
- □ 05 Communications and Media
- □ 06 Construction/Engineering
- □ 07 Consumer Sector/Consumer Packaged Goods
- □ 08 Education
- □ 09 Financial Services/Insurance
- □ 10 Government (civil)
- □ 11 Government (military)
- □ 12 Healthcare
- □ 13 High Technology Manufacturing, OEM
- □ 14 Integrated Software Vendor
- □ 15 Life Sciences (Biotech, Pharmaceuticals)
- □ 16 Mining
- □ 17 Retail/Wholesale/Distribution
- □ 18 Systems Integrator, VAR/VAD
- □ 19 Telecommunications
- □ 20 Travel and Transportation
- □ 21 Utilities (electric, gas, sanitation, water)
- □ 98 Other Business and Services

② WHICH OF THE FOLLOWING BEST DESCRIBES YOUR PRIMARY JOB FUNCTION? (check one only)
Corporate Management/Staff
- □ 01 Executive Management (President, Chair, CEO, CFO, Owner, Partner, Principal)
- □ 02 Finance/Administrative Management (VP/Director/ Manager/Controller, Purchasing, Administration)
- □ 03 Sales/Marketing Management (VP/Director/Manager)
- □ 04 Computer Systems/Operations Management (CIO/VP/Director/ Manager MIS, Operations)
IS/IT Staff
- □ 05 Systems Development/ Programming Management
- □ 06 Systems Development/ Programming Staff
- □ 07 Consulting
- □ 08 DBA/Systems Administrator
- □ 09 Education/Training
- □ 10 Technical Support Director/Manager
- □ 11 Other Technical Management/Staff
- □ 98 Other

③ WHAT IS YOUR CURRENT PRIMARY OPERATING PLATFORM? (select all that apply)
- □ 01 Digital Equipment UNIX
- □ 02 Digital Equipment VAX VMS
- □ 03 HP UNIX
- □ 04 IBM AIX
- □ 05 IBM UNIX
- □ 06 Java
- □ 07 Linux
- □ 08 Macintosh
- □ 09 MS-DOS
- □ 10 MVS
- □ 11 NetWare
- □ 12 Network Computing
- □ 13 OpenVMS
- □ 14 SCO UNIX
- □ 15 Sequent DYNIX/ptx
- □ 16 Sun Solaris/SunOS
- □ 17 SVR4
- □ 18 UnixWare
- □ 19 Windows
- □ 20 Windows NT
- □ 21 Other UNIX
- □ 98 Other
- 99 □ None of the above

④ DO YOU EVALUATE, SPECIFY, RECOMMEND, OR AUTHORIZE THE PURCHASE OF ANY OF THE FOLLOWING? (check all that apply)
- □ 01 Hardware
- □ 02 Software
- □ 03 Application Development Tools
- □ 04 Database Products
- □ 05 Internet or Intranet Products
- 99 □ None of the above

⑤ IN YOUR JOB, DO YOU USE OR PLAN TO PURCHASE ANY OF THE FOLLOWING PRODUCTS? (check all that apply)
Software
- □ 01 Business Graphics
- □ 02 CAD/CAE/CAM
- □ 03 CASE
- □ 04 Communications
- □ 05 Database Management
- □ 06 File Management
- □ 07 Finance
- □ 08 Java
- □ 09 Materials Resource Planning
- □ 10 Multimedia Authoring
- □ 11 Networking
- □ 12 Office Automation
- □ 13 Order Entry/Inventory Control
- □ 14 Programming
- □ 15 Project Management
- □ 16 Scientific and Engineering
- □ 17 Spreadsheets
- □ 18 Systems Management
- □ 19 Workflow

Hardware
- □ 20 Macintosh
- □ 21 Mainframe
- □ 22 Massively Parallel Processing
- □ 23 Minicomputer
- □ 24 PC
- □ 25 Network Computer
- □ 26 Symmetric Multiprocessing
- □ 27 Workstation
Peripherals
- □ 28 Bridges/Routers/Hubs/Gateways
- □ 29 CD-ROM Drives
- □ 30 Disk Drives/Subsystems
- □ 31 Modems
- □ 32 Tape Drives/Subsystems
- □ 33 Video Boards/Multimedia
Services
- □ 34 Application Service Provider
- □ 35 Consulting
- □ 36 Education/Training
- □ 37 Maintenance
- □ 38 Online Database Services
- □ 39 Support
- □ 40 Technology-Based Training
- □ 98 Other
- 99 □ None of the above

⑥ WHAT ORACLE PRODUCTS ARE IN USE AT YOUR SITE? (check all that apply)
Oracle E-Business Suite
- □ 01 Oracle Marketing
- □ 02 Oracle Sales
- □ 03 Oracle Order Fulfillment
- □ 04 Oracle Supply Chain Management
- □ 05 Oracle Procurement
- □ 06 Oracle Manufacturing
- □ 07 Oracle Maintenance Management
- □ 08 Oracle Service
- □ 09 Oracle Contracts
- □ 10 Oracle Projects
- □ 11 Oracle Financials
- □ 12 Oracle Human Resources
- □ 13 Oracle Interaction Center
- □ 14 Oracle Communications/Utilities (modules)
- □ 15 Oracle Public Sector/University (modules)
- □ 16 Oracle Financial Services (modules)
Server/Software
- □ 17 Oracle9*i*
- □ 18 Oracle9*i* Lite
- □ 19 Oracle8*i*
- □ 20 Other Oracle database
- □ 21 Oracle9*i* Application Server
- □ 22 Oracle9*i* Application Server Wireless
- □ 23 Oracle Small Business Suite

Tools
- □ 24 Oracle Developer Suite
- □ 25 Oracle Discoverer
- □ 26 Oracle JDeveloper
- □ 27 Oracle Migration Workbench
- □ 28 Oracle9*i*/AS Portal
- □ 29 Oracle Warehouse Builder
Oracle Services
- □ 30 Oracle Outsourcing
- □ 31 Oracle Consulting
- □ 32 Oracle Education
- □ 33 Oracle Support
- □ 98 Other
- 99 □ None of the above

⑦ WHAT OTHER DATABASE PRODUCTS ARE IN USE AT YOUR SITE? (check all that apply)
- □ 01 Access
- □ 02 Baan
- □ 03 dbase
- □ 04 Gupta
- □ 05 IBM DB2
- □ 06 Informix
- □ 07 Ingres
- □ 98 Other
- □ 08 Microsoft Access
- □ 09 Microsoft SQL Server
- □ 10 PeopleSoft
- □ 11 Progress
- □ 12 SAP
- □ 13 Sybase
- □ 14 VSAM
- 99 □ None of the above

⑧ WHAT OTHER APPLICATION SERVER PRODUCTS ARE IN USE AT YOUR SITE? (check all that apply)
- □ 01 BEA
- □ 02 IBM
- □ 03 Sybase
- □ 04 Sun
- □ 05 Other

⑨ DURING THE NEXT 12 MONTHS, HOW MUCH DO YOU ANTICIPATE YOUR ORGANIZATION WILL SPEND ON COMPUTER HARDWARE, SOFTWARE, PERIPHERALS, AND SERVICES FOR YOUR LOCATION? (check only one)
- □ 01 Less than $10,000
- □ 02 $10,000 to $49,999
- □ 03 $50,000 to $99,999
- □ 04 $100,000 to $499,999
- □ 05 $500,000 to $999,999
- □ 06 $1,000,000 and over

⑩ WHAT IS YOUR COMPANY'S YEARLY SALES REVENUE? (please choose one)
- □ 01 $500,000,000 and above
- □ 02 $100,000,000 to $500,000,000
- □ 03 $50,000,000 to $100,000,000
- □ 04 $5,000,000 to $50,000,000
- □ 05 $1,000,000 to $5,000,000

100103